AMERICA'S
WAR ON
CHRISTIANITY

IN GOD WE TRUST

BRAD O'LEARY

AMERICA'S WAR ON CHRISTIANITY

WND Books

America's War on Christianity

WND Books

Published by WorldNetDaily

Washington, D.C.

Copyright © 2010
Brad O'Leary

All rights reserved. No part of this book may be reproduced in any form or by any means, electronic, mechanical, photocopying, scanning, or otherwise, without permission in writing from the publisher, except by a reviewer who may quote brief passages in a review.

Jacket design by Linda Daly
Interior design by Neuwirth & Associates, Inc.

WND Books are distributed to the trade by:
Midpoint Trade Books
27 West 20th Street, Suite 1102
New York, NY 10011

WND Books are available at special discounts for bulk purchases. WND Books, Inc. also publishes books in electronic formats. For more information call (541) 474-1776 or visit www.wndbooks.com.

First Edition

ISBN 13 Digit: 978-1-935071-24-2

Library of Congress information available

Printed in the United States of America

10 9 8 7 6 5 4 3 2 1

CONTENTS

FOREWORD

And yet the same revolutionary beliefs for which our forebears fought are still at issue around the globe—the belief that the rights of man come not from the generosity of the state, but from the hand of God.

—*President John F. Kennedy,*
Inaugural Address, January 20, 1961

THE JUDEO-CHRISTIAN VALUES upon which America was founded are under attack. Secular extremists and antireligious forces are on a public mission to remove religious faith from our history and national consciousness. These forces claim that America's founding and system of government don't have anything to do with religion—and never should. Their goal is to replace the power of God with the power of government—a government which they control.

I wrote this book to expose the many ways God and Christianity are under attack in America. The unadulterated words of America's founders and leaders prove that God and religious faith are seamlessly intertwined with our nation's past and present. The future, however, will depend on the outcomes of various battles taking place within our ongoing culture war at the federal, state, and local levels. I also wrote this book because our current president, Barack Obama, declared that America is not a Christian nation.

There is a small, yet vocal minority bent on expunging the phrase "In God We Trust" from everything remotely deemed "public." These are secular extremists who promote the "separation between Church and State" fallacy. These mistaken disciples of secular humanism fail to understand that our Founding Fathers, in the very First Amendment to the U.S. Constitution, sought to guard our freedom *of* religion, not guarantee us freedom *from* religion. We all have the freedom to believe, or not believe, as we wish. But to whitewash over the religious and biblical foundations that gave birth to our country, our rule of law, and our liberty is to rewrite history in a way that would make only the most paranoid tyrant proud.

"Thinkers" on the secular left often cite the musings of eighteenth-century philosopher Immanuel Kant as the intellectual foundation for their arguments. Among Kant's greatest hits are quotations like, "He who has made great moral progress ceases to pray," or, "The death of dogma is the birth of morality." Kant refers to religion and God as "superstition" and "folly." These "thinkers" believe that true enlightenment and freedom can only come from an atheistic—or at the very least—agnostic society. They ignore the many lessons in history that show, beyond a doubt, that tyranny is only possible without religion, and religion is the greatest enemy of tyranny.

Yet it is the philosophy of Kant that echoes throughout the halls of our higher education institutions. God and religion are ridiculed. Government programs, state welfare, higher taxes, stiffer regulations, and penalties—these are all revered as "logical," "right," and "good." Kantian socialism, which is at the core of communist and totalitarian philosophy, is presented to our nation's budding young minds as a noble endeavor that just might some day, if implemented correctly, lead to the perfection of the human condition. Few are the minds that survive four undergraduate years of this indoctrination.

Why ridicule God? Because when man looks to God for salvation, he searches within himself for his own ability and morality. When man is forbidden from looking to God for salvation, he must fixate on the State for everything he needs.

Thus, the current war is divided into two camps. On one side, we have religion and freedom. On the other side, we have atheism and totalitarianism. Both sides have scored victories in the ongoing struggle.

For example, in 2007 a seventeen-year-old boy from Ohio wrote his congressman and requested a flag be flown over the U.S. Capitol to honor his grandfather for his "love of God, country, and family." The Capitol architect refused to make the religious dedication, citing a rule against "religious expressions." Thankfully, after much controversy, this rule was reversed and the Ohio boy's request was honored.

Since a landmark decision in 1962, the U.S. Supreme Court has consistently ruled against any prayer in public schools—even banning students from publicly praying before the start of high school football games. However, our most public of institutions, the U.S. Congress, begins each day with a prayer when the body is in session. We should wonder how much longer this tradition will last.

The Capitol Visitors Center, which opened in December 2008, was built with more than $600 million from American taxpayers. According to polls, nine in ten Americans believe in God. Still, nowhere in the Capitol Visitors Center will you find a reference to God—not even the slightest historical reference to our nation's Christian heritage makes an appearance. Instead, the center is shrine to the power of government, man, and secular causes.

In cities and towns across America, public nativity scenes are treated like pornography every Christmastime, and the phrase "Merry Christmas" has become a veritable slur. More recently, in 2010, the city of Davenport, Iowa tried to rename Good Friday—the most solemn day on the Christian Calendar—"Spring Holiday."

It is baffling why any American would not seek to commemorate our nation's Christian heritage, regardless of creed—whether they are Christian, Jewish, or even Muslim or Atheist. The freedom we all enjoy is deeply rooted in the Judeo-Christian values that our Founders and leaders have practiced.

I hope the factual accounts in this book, which document the current secular war on Christianity, serve as a warning to all who cherish freedom. My hope is that in the future, America's religious heritage be celebrated by all—not bound, gagged, and locked in a closet.

AMERICA'S
WAR ON
CHRISTIANITY

1.

THE GOVERNMENT AND CHRISTIANITY

> [T]his notion that's peddled by the religious right—that they are oppressed—is not true. Sometimes it's a cynical ploy to move their agenda ahead. The classic example being that somehow secularists are trying to eliminate Christmas, which strikes me as some kind of manufactured controversy.
>
> —President Barack Obama,
> Interview with StreetProphets.com, January 16, 2007

A FUNNY THING happened on the way to Georgetown University, where Barack Obama, newly minted forty-fourth president of the United States, was to give an address in April 2009. You might call it the "Georgetown Cover-up."

Besides all the obligatory security measures that attend any presidential visitation, the prestigious Catholic institution in Washington, D.C. also found itself in the awkward position of having to cover up the very religious symbols that represent its core beliefs, out of deference to its First Visitor. While that may be just mildly curious to those who have been well conditioned in this day and age to keeping their religious and political opinions to themselves, it would have flabbergasted the Founding Fathers. They might well have found this kind of bowdlerizing to be—well, downright un-American.

Take Thomas Jefferson, America's third president, the very one who originated the expression "separation of church and state." Supposedly the least religious of the lot, Jefferson himself regularly participated in religious services—held *in the Capitol Building*. In fact, the Capitol hosted weekly worship services for decades, often including Sunday school, until 1866, when there were plenty of denominational churches in the city to attend. The very Liberty Bell that pealed in Philadelphia to proclaim independence on July 4, 1776, was named for the biblical inscription from Leviticus 25:10 emblazoned around it: "Proclaim liberty throughout the land, to all the inhabitants thereof."

Deacon Keith Fournier points out that Jefferson truly understood the sources of our liberty. His own words, inscribed in the Jefferson Memorial, seem almost to portend a time such as ours when that source would no longer be assumed: "God who gave us life gave us liberty. Can the liberties of a nation be secure when we have removed a conviction that these liberties are the gift of God?"[1]

One can only try to imagine Jefferson's incredulity if he could have witnessed how inimical the American state had become to faith and the church by 2009. And it wasn't the church that moved. It was the American state that lost its way—coerced, cajoled, and co-opted by a host of special interests that Washington, Adams, and Jefferson could never have foreseen in their wildest dreams. It's only when you try to enumerate the many theaters where this culture war has flared that you can even begin to get a sense of the enormity of the battle that has been thrust upon Jefferson's republic in these latter days. The following are at least some of the more public battle lines and skirmishes that have befallen it.

In God We Trust

It's a good thing the words of the national motto, "In God We Trust," were engraved in stone over the Speaker's rostrum in the U.S. House of Representatives. They'll last longer that way. The new $621 million Capitol Visitors Center omitted both "In God We Trust" and the Pledge of Allegiance, until some congressmen on the House Administration Committee intervened.[2] And when the U.S. Mint began issuing a new series of presidential $1 coins in 2007, nowhere on either side appeared the words "In God We Trust," a mainstay on our coinage since Civil War days. The words were inscribed instead on the edge of these coins. Responding to constituents, Congress passed a bill restoring the motto to the front of the coins.

There has been, in fact, an ongoing legal battle for many years to get "In God We Trust" rescinded as the national motto. In the 1990s the national Freedom from Religion Foundation (FFRF) waged an unsuccessful legal battle all the way to the U.S. Supreme Court to have the motto struck down as unconstitutional. More recently, noted atheist Dr. Michael Newdow lost a similar federal court challenge in 2006. In both instances, federal judges ruled that "In God We Trust" was more a patriotic expression than a religious declaration.

It was certainly a religious intent, however, on the part of the Reverend M. R. Watkinson, a Pennsylvania minister, who first urged the adoption of a similar expression to Treasury Secretary Salmon P. Chase, a fellow believer, during the Civil War. Watkinson wrote:

> This would make a beautiful coin, to which no possible citizen could object. This would relieve us from the ignominy of heathenism. This would place us openly under the Divine protection we have personally claimed. From my heart I have felt our national shame in disowning God as not the least of our present national disasters.

It's worth visiting the U.S. Treasury Department's Web site to read the rest of this inspiring story.[3]

Pledge of Allegiance

No doubt Watkinson would have felt a special kinship with the Reverend George MacPherson Docherty, a transplanted Scotsman who succeeded the famous Peter

Marshall as pastor of the prestigious New York Avenue Presbyterian Church in Washington, D.C., down the street from the White House. Various presidents from the time of Abraham Lincoln have frequented its pews. In 1954, it was President Dwight Eisenhower, and Docherty seized the opportunity to preach a sermon that would move the commander in chief to press successfully for the addition of two simple words to the Pledge of Allegiance—"under God"—through an act of Congress that same year. Docherty argued that without acknowledging the Creator, the pledge missed its American distinctiveness:

> To omit the words "under God" is to omit the definitive character of the American way of life. What the Declaration [of Independence] says, in effect, is that no state church shall exist in this land. This is separation of church and state. It is not and never was meant to be a separation of religion and life. . . . There was something missing in this pledge, and that which was missing was the characteristic and definitive factor in the American way of life. Indeed, apart from the phrase "the United States of America," this could be the pledge of any republic. In fact, I could hear little Muscovites repeat a similar pledge to their hammer-and-sickle flag with equal solemnity.[4]

Various parties, including Michael Newdow, have attempted unsuccessfully to have the pledge declared unconstitutional for violating the Establishment Clause.

Federal appeals courts have disagreed on this point, and the only time it came before the U.S. Supreme Court in 2004, the justices threw it out on a technicality rather than deal with the Constitutional issue. The justices ruled that Newdow lacked standing as the noncustodial parent to sue on behalf of his daughter. So, the last word undoubtedly has yet to be spoken. But the First Amendment Center, a strong secular advocate in the church-state debate, has stated: "The question that will likely resurface is whether the inclusion of the words 'under God' violates the Establishment Clause. However, given the opinions of the justices in Newdow, an Establishment Clause challenge to the pledge would face some high hurdles."[5]

There has been an apparent reluctance on the part of some federal judges, at least, to let themselves get in the way of God and country. As part of this dance, some have even denied that the pledge's "under God" phrase is really religious at all, but rather secular, ceremonial, or patriotic. Reverend Docherty, who started the whole issue, would have strenuously disagreed. To read Docherty's historic sermon in its entirety, visit the New York Avenue church's online archive.[6]

Still, the Freedom from Religion Foundation filed a federal lawsuit to try to stop the engraving of both "In God We Trust" and "One Nation Under God" in the new Capitol Visitors Center. Annie Laurie Gaylor, FFRF co-president, asserted that the mottoes were junk history, contrived in the 1950s as "anti-communist" measures. "Boy, are they misinformed," she told *USA Today*, which did not bother—or know—to correct Gaylor's own junk history.[7] For "In God We Trust," at least, she was off by about a century.

Ten Commandments

Legal consensus has thus far eluded the federal judiciary on the question of whether displaying the Ten Commandments on public property constitutes a prohibited sectarian religious expression or is merely a secular acknowledgment of the history of our best moral and legal principles. The most celebrated case occurred in Alabama where Judge Roy Moore, a Bible-believing Christian, arranged for a 2.5-ton Vermont granite monument to be installed in the state courthouse in 2003, a month after becoming chief justice of the Alabama Supreme Court. Moore declared on the occasion:

> Today a cry has gone out across our land for the acknowledgment of that God upon whom this nation and our laws were founded. . . . May this day mark the restoration of the moral foundation of law to our people and the return to the knowledge of God in our land.[8]

Rather, it resulted in Judge Moore's own removal from office after he disregarded a federal court order to remove the display. A CNN-*USA Today*-Gallup poll at the time, however, found 77 percent of Americans surveyed disapproved of the federal judge's order to remove the monument in the first place.[9]

In Oklahoma, federal judges have ordered Haskell County officials to remove a Ten Commandments display outside the county courthouse.

In June 2009, a federal judge ordered two southern Kentucky counties to remove copies of the Ten Commandments in courthouses and pay more than $400,000 to the American Civil Liberties Union and citizens who successfully challenged the displays. That case remains under appeal.[10]

Crosses

War memorials displaying crosses on public property in honor of our nation's fallen fighters are under legal attack because the cross is also a Christian religious symbol. The battle extends as far as the Mojave Desert, where a plywood box has been built around a seven-foot veterans' memorial cross to shield it from view in the wilderness until the matter can be sorted out. The U.S. Supreme Court has agreed to hear the case.

Probably the most notorious case is in San Diego, where a legal fight over a twenty-nine-foot Korean War veteran memorial cross has been raging for twenty years, thanks to the American Civil Liberties Union, which sued in 1989. After the first adverse ruling from a federal judge, the city attempted to fix the problem by asking voters to approve transfer of the property to a private organization while appealing the ruling. To absolutely no one's surprise, the notoriously liberal Ninth U.S. Circuit Court of Appeals upheld the original injunction. The ACLU returned to district court and convinced the original judge not only to block the land transfer, but to order that the cross be dismantled.

Local veterans and other defenders of the memorial refused to give up. They won the support of Rep. Duncan Hunter (R-CA), who sponsored a successful bill to transfer the property to federal control. The ACLU, however, was equally adamant and started the litigation all over again, losing the first round at the district court—which sends it back to the Ninth Circuit. This case, too, appears bound for the Supreme Court no matter the outcome at the appellate level.

In Chesapeake, Virginia, officials ordered Christians in 2007 to remove a cross that they deemed "offensive" from a booth the group was permitted to set up in a public park following an Independence Day parade.[11]

At Virginia's College of William and Mary, founded in 1693 as the second college in the colonies, the administration decided to remove the antique bronze cross from the historic Wren Chapel in 2007, after receiving a single complaint to make it less "faith-specific." After the inevitable furor ensuing from alumni and students, the college compromised by moving the cross into a glass display case at the front of the chapel, like an ancient relic from a bygone era.[12]

Hate Crimes

Secular extremists have long pushed for so-called hate crimes laws (which are actually "thought crimes" laws) to provide additional criminal penalties for crimes committed against homosexuals and transgendered people. However, many refer to such a national hate/thought crimes bill as the "Pedophile Protection Act" because in the process of extending special federal protection to individuals on the basis of sexual orientation and gender identity, the majority in the U.S. House has refused to exclude any of the 547 forms of sexual deviancy or "paraphilias" listed by the American Psychiatric Association, including pedophilia.[13] Nor would the majority agree to extend those same "enhanced penalty" protections to military veterans attacked because of their service—as happened in Little Rock, Arkansas, when a Muslim convert shot and killed a twenty-four-year-old Army recruiter in June 2009, reportedly for ideological reasons.

In October 2009, the secular extremists got their wish. The Democrat-led Congress passed and President Obama signed the "Hate Crimes Prevention Act." This new law adds homosexuals and transsexuals to the list of uber-protected citizens under existing federal Hate Crimes law. The Act passed as an amendment to the National Defense Authorization Act. In other words, a vote against the Hate Crimes bill would have been a vote against fund-

ing our troops in Iraq and Afghanistan. Such is the under-
handed way Congress conducts business.

The Act effectively criminalizes any speech that hatred
incites and leads to violence against any of the special
classes of citizens (homosexuals, transsexuals, etc.) protected under the law.

Democratic champions of the bill claim a provision in
the law specifically protects "a person's exercise of religion, speech, expression, or association" as proof that the
bill doesn't eviscerate the First Amendment. However,
this is intentionally misleading.

The bill's provision in its entirety reads:

> Nor shall anything in this division . . . be construed
> or applied in a manner that *substantially* burdens a
> person's exercise of religion, speech, expression, or
> association, *unless the Government demonstrates
> that application of the burden to the person is in fur-
> therance of a compelling governmental interest and is
> the least restrictive means of furthering that compel-
> ling governmental interest.* (Emphasis added.)

That is a big "unless." And what constitutes "sub-
stantially"? The bill actually says that Americans' right to
freedom of speech, thought, and religion is still sacred . . .
unless the government decides it isn't.

How might this play out in practice? Say someone
assaults a gay person and it's determined that the

perpetrator is an avid fan of Rush Limbaugh. And it's then discovered that Limbaugh had recently been railing against Hate Crimes legislation, or gay marriage, or another gay issue. Limbaugh could then be prosecuted under this law if the government determines there is a "compelling interest" to do so. The same scenario holds true for a Christian preacher who speaks out against homosexuality—or anyone with the public's ear.

American voters, according to an October 2009 Zogby International/O'Leary Report Poll, aren't too keen on the new Hate Crimes law. (The poll surveyed 3,544 voters, was conducted October 23–26, and has a margin of error of 1.7 percentage points). The poll asked:

> The U.S. House of Representatives recently passed a "Hate Crimes" bill that would make assault based on sexual orientation or perceived gender identity a felony. As it is currently written, the bill would also allow the prosecution of people whose speech allegedly influences others to commit hate crimes. Some experts believe this could lead to serious infringements on free speech, as well as the prosecution of religious preachers, talk show hosts or political activists who speak against homosexuality or transsexuals. Others say the bill is an effort to try and stop people from committing such crimes in the future. Do you agree or disagree with the Hate Crimes bill?

A plurality of Americans (47 percent) said they disagree with the Hate Crimes bill, while only 38 percent agree with it. A majority of Independent voters (55 percent) disagree with the bill, and just 29 percent agree with it.

Peter Sprigg of the Family Research Council prefers to call them "thought crimes" laws, noting that violent attacks by themselves are already illegal. "What's needed is not a new law, but the strict enforcement of existing laws—to protect *all* Americans equally." As Sprigg notes:

> In fact, the very term "hate crime" is offensive in this context, in that it implies that mere disapproval of homosexual behavior constitutes a form of "hate" equivalent to racial bigotry. . . . The rhetoric of pro-homosexual activists makes it clear that their goal is not just to protect homosexuals from violence, but to protect them from criticism altogether by silencing those who seek to discourage homosexual behavior.[14]

This new hate crimes law will have an inevitable chilling effect on the pulpits in America, as pastors will have to think twice about addressing the biblical view of homosexuality. Merely one person's word blaming such a sermon for a subsequent act of violence could result in prosecution. A fundamental flaw of all hate crimes laws, says Matt

Barber, is that they promote "unequal protection" of the laws in direct conflict with the Fourteenth Amendment to the U.S. Constitution. Barber, director of cultural affairs for Liberty Council and Liberty Alliance Action, wrote:

> Existing hate-crimes laws create a two-tiered justice system with first-class victims and second-class victims. Second-class victims—such as the elderly, veterans, the homeless or children—are explicitly denied the same resources, attention and justice given to those who are arbitrarily deemed to be first-class victims. This is as un-American as it is unfair.[15]

Jesus' Name

It is now possible in America to be arrested and charged with a misdemeanor for praying in the name of Jesus. Such was the case in Fredericksburg, Virginia, where the city adopted a penalty of disorderly conduct for anyone violating a city council ban on praying in Jesus' name in public meetings. The ban was upheld by the Fourth U.S. Circuit Court of Appeals. Retired Supreme Court Justice Sandra Day O'Connor, sitting in for the case, said the council acted reasonably to ban prayers that constituted "government speech." The U.S. Supreme Court left it right there, declining to hear the appeal.

Since the 1950s, Fredericksburg city council members had been praying on a rotating basis to open sessions. After minister Hashmel Turner joined the council in 2002, the ACLU and others began threatening to sue, and the council revised its policy to allow only "nondenominational prayers." Lawyers for the Rutherford Institute, which handles cases involving freedom of religious expression, filed suit, arguing that dictating the content of prayers violated the Establishment Clause of the Constitution as well as Turner's Free Exercise rights. Rutherford lost the first round at U.S. District Court. In its appeal, the institute asserted:

> Unquestionably, the city council's policy was aimed directly at Councilor Turner and his practice of closing prayer in the name of Jesus Christ . . . after the policy was adopted, other city council members were permitted to pray in the name of other deities and to utter prayers reflecting denominational influences . . . whereas councilor Turner was precluded from praying.[16]

Meanwhile, the non-denominational-prayer standard was adopted statewide as official policy in Virginia, prompting six of its seventeen state trooper chaplains to resign in protest of the new restriction. Gordon Klingenschmitt, a former Navy chaplain who has had his own struggles over praying in Jesus' name, called the Virginia trooper chaplains heroes "because they refused to deny Jesus when ordered to" by Democratic Governor Tim Kaine's administration. Klingenschmitt said the city of Fredericksburg, and then Justice O'Connor, in their shortsighted attempts to shut down free exercise, had ironically gone to the other extreme of religious establishment: "The Fredericksburg government violated everybody's rights by *establishing a nonsectarian religion* and requiring all prayers conform, or face punishment of exclusion"[17] (emphasis added).

Klingenschmitt was fined $3,000 and discharged from the Navy in 2007 for violating orders after he prayed in Jesus' name at a White House rally, capping a protracted battle over the issue. His stand on conscience was ultimately vindicated as Congress took note and passed legislation ordering the Navy to rescind these restrictions and allow chaplains to pray as their "conscience dictates." Klingenschmitt expressed gratitude that some good came from his own adversity. "My sacrifice purchased their freedom," he said. "My conscience is clear, the fight was worth it, and I'd do it all again."[18]

According to Rutherford founder John W. Whitehead, "There's a unitarian system of religion that's aimed at Christians. It boils down to that. We're seeing it all across the country, with council prayers, kids wanting to mention Jesus. What's going on here is it's generally a move in our government and military to set up a civil religion."[19]

"Spring Holiday"

Whitehead's warning about a "civil religion" slowly eroding and replacing Christianity was evident in Davenport,

Iowa, in 2010, just days before the most solemn day on the Christian calendar. Upon the recommendation of the Davenport Civil Rights Commission, City Administrator Craig Malin sent an advisory to all city employees announcing that "Good Friday" would henceforth be known as "Spring Holiday."

Christian employees of the city and union members with city contracts wasted no time expressing their outrage that Davenport would whitewash their faith so callously. According to City Council Alderman Bill Edmond, phones began "ringing off the hook" immediately after the "Spring Holiday" decree.

"People are genuinely upset because this is nothing but political correctness run amok," said Edmond. "The city council didn't know anything about the change. We were blind-sided and now we've got to clean this mess up. How do you tell people the city renamed a 2,000 year old holiday?"[20]

Davenport's Civil Rights Commission chairman, Tim Hart, trotted out the same tired and grossly erroneous line about why it was so necessary to stamp out a Christian holiday: "Our Constitution calls for a separation of church and state," he said. Perhaps Hart should put down his diversity training manual long enough to actually read our Constitution. Doing so might spare him more embarrassing episodes like this one.

Just days after the "Spring Holiday" announcement was made, it was rescinded, and "Good Friday" was restored.

Military Facilities

There was a time when men entering the United States' armed services—potentially to lay down their lives for their country—were encouraged to exercise their Christian faith, or any faith tradition they might observe. During World War II, President Franklin Roosevelt, though not specifically invoking the name of Christ, prayed over national airwaves for the success of the D-Day invasion and the war effort in a manner that today would surely unleash a torrent of protest:

> Almighty God: Our sons, pride of our Nation, this day have set upon a mighty endeavor, a struggle to preserve our Republic, *our religion*, and our civilization, and to set free a suffering humanity. . . . And, O Lord, give us Faith. Give us Faith in Thee; Faith in our sons; Faith in each other; Faith in our united crusade. Let not the keenness of our spirit ever be dulled. Let not the impacts of temporary events, of temporal matters of but fleeting moment, let not these deter us in our unconquerable purpose. With Thy blessing, we shall prevail over the unholy forces of our enemy.[21] (Emphasis added)

It wasn't Shintoism or the Baha'i faith that FDR had in mind with the phrase "our religion." It was America's Judeo-Christian beliefs, which have been a pillar of society since the nation's founding. Current attempts to deny, stifle, and eradicate them are a much more recent aberration. Still, today the official U.S. Military Code of Conduct (Article Six) states: "I will never forget that I am an American, fighting for freedom, responsible for my actions, and dedicated to the principles which made my country free. *I will trust in my God* and in the United States of America"[22] (emphasis added). Or in the case of Lackland Air Force Base in Florida, my "goddess." The base in recent years has hosted weekly meetings for practitioners of Wicca—witchcraft. It has nothing to do with Satan, insist these Wiccans. Rather, they practice a reverence of nature, worship of a fertility goddess, hedonism, and "group magic."[23]

If things are looking up for neo-pagans in the military, however, it's a rather different story for Christians. Military facilities, particularly the service academies, have become prime targets in recent years of anti-Christian forces in America. The American Civil Liberties Union and others have tried unsuccessfully, for example, to halt lunch prayers at the Naval Academy at Annapolis, Maryland.

Perhaps the most egregious case occurred in 2005 at the U.S. Air Force Academy in Colorado Springs, where a visiting antiwar Yale professor, the local newspaper, and Americans United for Separation of Church and State found common cause in beating back expressions of evangelical faith on the campus.

Chaplains were accused of going too far in proselytizing and talking too freely about hell and who's going there. Christian cadets were accused of calling non-Christians "heathens." (It was a joke.) Top brass were condemned for promoting participation in the National Day of Prayer. Churchgoing Falcons football coach Fisher DeBerry was attacked for promoting pregame prayers and posting a banner in the locker room, declaring, "I am a Christian first and last. . . . I am a member of Team Jesus Christ." Those weren't actually DeBerry's words; they were the familiar Competitor's Creed of the Fellowship of Christian Athletes. Nevertheless, DeBerry was ordered to take it down. Focus on the Family's *Citizen* magazine discovered such serious distortions in this ginned-up controversy that it termed the attacks a "smear."[24]

A Pentagon investigation, demanded by the news media, Americans United, and the Anti-Defamation League, found that much of this religious activity at the Air Force Academy had been voluntarily instigated by the cadets themselves, such as distributing fliers promoting Mel Gibson's *The Passion of the Christ* movie. Officials were largely cleared of wrongdoing, although the commandant, Brigadier General Johnny Weida, was passed over for his next promotion. The biggest casualty was public expression of faith. New Air Force guidelines restricted public prayer to special occasions (no staff meetings or sporting events), and then only the brief, "non-sectarian" variety—i.e., no Jesus.

Meanwhile, some in Congress were growing increasingly uncomfortable with the direction things were taking. One was Rep. Walter Jones (R-NC) a senior member of the House Armed Services Committee, who has championed legislation to expand freedom of religious expression at the service academies. Jones' concerns echoed those of Klingenschmitt and Whitehead. "Officially inhibiting or defining what chaplains can and cannot say in effect establishes an official religion and burdens our military's chaplains' right of free speech," he said.

Jones, who is Catholic, said he was especially moved by an Air Force chaplain who told him, "'Congressman, I hope you will do something about this. I cannot tell you how many times'—and he started crying—'I've gone back to my office and got down on my knees and asked God to forgive me because I was afraid to say the name of His Son when I closed my prayer.'" Jones said. "I think there's going to come a time, if we don't draw the line in the sand now, that we will lose the right to practice freely what we believe."[25]

Anti-Catholic Measures

A line has been drawn in the state of Connecticut, where but for some eleventh-hour outbreaks of common sense, an unprecedented intrusion into church affairs nearly became law. It's a rather shocking story, tainted by bad blood and alleged political paybacks. It was disturbing enough to provoke Bishop William Lori to abandon protocol and outright accuse state officials of corruption by "special interests and back-room deals."[26]

It apparently started with a bill to require all hospitals to provide emergency contraception (chemical abortion) to rape victims, with *no exemption for Catholic facilities*. Although the Bridgeport Diocese fought the legislation for two years, state lawmakers prevailed and it became law in 2007.

A couple of Connecticut state legislators next sponsored a measure taking direct aim at the diocese. If successful, the bill would require Roman Catholic parishes to reorganize their governing structures and replace priests with lay leaders for financial oversight. It was an unprecedented state intrusion, dictating a board of directors of seven to thirteen lay members. It specifically barred priests, bishops, and archbishops from any voting authority and even specified the board's duties and how often it would meet.[27]

Outraged Catholics were encouraged to contact their elected representatives to fight the bill. At one point, 4,000 Catholics rallied in the state capitol to declare their opposition. The American Society for the Defense of Tradition, Family, and Property denounced the "persecutory character" of SB 1098. "This bill, moreover, is a thinly veiled attempt to silence the Catholic Church on the important issues of the day, such as same-sex marriage." Lawmakers denied any connection between the financial oversight legislation and the church's opposition to same-sex marriage. But to believe that required also believing that it was just a coincidence that the sponsors of SB 1098—Sen. Andrew J. McDonald and Rep. Michael P. Lawlor—were also key advocates for the legalization of same-sex marriage. Sen. Michael McLachlan, for one, wasn't buying it: "The real purpose of this bill is payback to the bishops and pastors of the Roman Catholic Church in Connecticut for opposing gay marriage."[28]

The escalation continued. The diocese next received notification from the Connecticut Office of State Ethics that it was being investigated for possible violations of state lobbying laws for its political activities and could be fined $10,000 and potentially subjected to other criminal charges. If forced to register as a lobbyist, the diocese would be subject to other reporting requirements and audits, and officials would be required to wear identification badges in the Capitol. The diocese sued in federal court to block the action. Declared Bishop Lori:

> This new action cannot be seen as anything other than an attempt to muzzle the church and subject our right of free speech to government review and regulation. This government action tramples on the First Amendment freedoms of speech, assembly and religion, and should shock the conscience of all citizens of the Constitution State."[29]

Eventually, cooler heads prevailed. Support for SB 1098 withered. Attorney General Richard Blumenthal asked the Office of State Ethics to back off, citing "profound and serious constitutional issues." He said the diocese's actions in communicating with its members and even rallying expressions of protest were "clearly and unquestionably" protected by the First Amendment.[30] The diocese then dropped its lawsuit against the ethics commission.

It was a near miss, produced by a combination of circumstances not exclusive to the Northeast that could only too easily happen elsewhere. In fact, it has.

The San Francisco Board of Supervisors—with the explicit blessing of the federal judiciary—has condemned the Catholic Church as "hateful" and "callous" for its opposition to gay marriage. It passed a resolution condemning the Vatican as a "foreign country" and its teachings on homosexuality as "insulting" and "defamatory." It said the church's special concern for gay adoption was "doing violence" to children subjected to these conditions. The Ninth U.S. Circuit Court of Appeals specifically upheld the Board of Supervisors' condemnation of the Catholic church as "well within" its rights to denounce discrimination for "the general welfare of society."[31]

Considering the trends, don't look for this sort of anti-Christian behavior to go away any time soon.

"Unnecessary Noise"

Sometimes it's hard to believe such things happen in America today, but increasingly they do. Not that many years ago, for example, it was commonplace in American towns and cities to mark the hour with the pealing of church bells. Today that might get you arrested. At least, that's what happened in Phoenix, Arizona, where Bishop Rick Painter was threatened with jail for ringing the electronic chimes at Cathedral of Christ the King Church. A municipal judge gave Painter three years probation and a suspended ten-day jail sentence for violating city noise ordinances by creating "an unreasonably loud, disturbing, and unnecessary noise."[32]

The church now is allowed to ring the bells only on Sunday mornings and a court-ordered list of select religious holidays. The Alliance Defense Fund, which is handling Painter's legal appeal, noted that the church bells produced fewer decibels than an ice cream truck, which the city does permit. Said ADF senior legal counsel Erik Stanley:

> In a busy neighborhood full of sirens, heavy traffic, and loud motorcycles, these chimes are a sound of peace that do not exceed the noise level of an average conversation. Certainly, that should be at least as acceptable as the sound of an ice cream truck. . . . It's ridiculous to be sentenced to jail and probation for doing what churches have traditionally done throughout history. Christians shouldn't be punished for exercising their faith publicly.[33]

In Michigan police threatened to arrest musicians at Faith Baptist Church in Waterford Township for disorderly conduct for music considered too loud. The church said police entered the sanctuary at least twice, including once during a Sunday service, without a warrant. The Thomas More Law Center, which represented the church in a First Amendment federal lawsuit against the township, said during one Wednesday night youth service, uniformed police burst into the church's sanctuary. The township prosecutor ordered the officers to take the names and addresses of all the young people in the praise and worship band so they could be charged with disorderly conduct.

Richard Thompson, president and chief counsel of the Law Center, observed, "Uniformed police officers entering a church during religious services and young church members being threatened with prosecution is something that happens in Communist China—not in America."[34]

Sometimes these stories have a happy ending, but only after Christians have gone to the trouble of standing up for their rights as Americans. Fort Macon State Park officials in North Carolina ordered Grace Baptist Church members to stop sharing the gospel with other park visitors—or be prosecuted for holding a meeting or speech without a permit. When a complaint to the state Division of Parks and Recreation didn't produce results, Liberty Counsel filed a federal lawsuit challenging the constitutionality of the permit requirement. Only then did the state back off, agreeing to a settlement including payment of attorney's fees.

"Permits for speech are prior restraints on speech, and in most cases such restraints are unconstitutional," said Matt Staver, founder of Liberty Counsel and dean of

Liberty University School of Law. "It makes no sense to require a single individual to obtain a license to speak to another person in a public park."[35]

In San Diego, Pastor David Jones and his wife, Mary, were issued a citation barring them from holding Tuesday night Bible studies in their home. Otherwise, they would have to spend hundreds of dollars and apply for a major use permit from the county or pay big fines. The incident might be chalked up to a misunderstanding on the part of an overzealous code enforcer, but no such actions were brought against people holding poker nights or Tupperware parties in their homes. Only after a deluge of bad publicity and a demand letter from the Western Center for Law & Policy, did the county see the error of its ways. The citation was withdrawn, and the Joneses were given an official apology for the "unfortunate events."[36]

And sometimes anti-Christian bias seems to be perpetrated not just with malice aforethought, but almost as an in-your-face flaunting of political muscle. Sen. Jim DeMint (R-SC) got a taste of that in February 2009 when he tried to amend the Obama stimulus package to remove an anti-faith provision. This section denied stimulus funds for improvements to any facilities "used for sectarian instruction, religious worship, or a school or department of divinity." Think of the many public schools in America, for example, that earn extra income from weekend rentals to churches or have Bible clubs under the Equal Access laws. DeMint's amendment was soundly rejected in a largely party-line vote.

"This bill shuts off secular colleges from permitting religious services on campus if they receive any federal money from this stimulus bill," according to the Traditional Values Coalition. Executive Director Andrea Lafferty predicted, "This is just the beginning of aggressive anti-Christian bigotry that we will see over the next four years. We suffered a significant defeat to our First Amendment's guarantee of religious freedom and free speech today."[37]

War on Christmas

Years ago, the good people of Garfield Heights, Ohio, a suburb of Cleveland, discovered a way to get secular extremists off their backs at Christmastime when complaints began over a public nativity scene: They simply inserted a Santa Claus figure into the Holy Family tableau and—*voilà!*—it was no longer a strictly religious symbol, but merely a festive seasonal representation.

Several years later, the good people of the Washington, D.C., suburb of Vienna, Virginia, tried a similar move with reindeer, Santas, and snowmen. This was inspired by a 1985 Supreme Court ruling known as the "reindeer rule" or "plastic reindeer test," a balancing of sacred and secular images, so as not to imply that the state is endorsing religion. But this time the ACLU fought on anyway, arguing that the nativity was still the central focus of the display. A federal judge agreed, and the nativity scene was yanked. The next year, protesters showed up at the site with their own nativity display, singing Christmas carols and carrying banners. One read: "The ACLU is jealous of manger scenes because it doesn't have three wise men or a virgin in its organization."[38]

But that kind of feistiness is uncommon. More often the good people simply take the easier course and capitulate to the demands by shutting down or removing the alleged object of offense. No one needs that kind of grief, especially at Christmas. This can lead, however, to some truly odd situations, such as Christmas parades open to everybody—except Christ and Christians. That was the case in Denver in 2004, when Faith Bible Chapel was banned from having its float in the annual Parade of Lights because of its overtly religious theme. Instead, the parade featured homosexual American Indians, Kung Fu artisans, belly dancers, and Santa Claus. In a masterpiece of understatement, Pastor George Morrison responded, "I think there's an agenda that is anti-Christian."[39]

Again, it's a trend that seems to be picking up steam. Sometimes the battles go beyond courtrooms and city halls and reach literally into the manger itself. Each year, dozens of communities experience "Baby Jesus theft," a literal robbing of the cradle. No doubt many of these thefts are youthful pranks, but others are clearly something else entirely, judging by other acts, such as vandalism, violent damage to the Christ child, and obscenities left marking the scene.[40] Some churches have gone to the extreme of protecting their manger babies with computer chips or GPS locators.

Meanwhile, Christians have started to become more assertive, willing to exercise the power of the purse by shunning retailers who won't acknowledge Christmas but want the Christmas business. Increasingly there may be a price tag attached to these antireligion policies. Voters in Mustang, Oklahoma, vented their frustration over the school superintendent's decision to remove a nativity scene from an elementary school by voting down $11 million worth of bond issues for the school district.[41]

Culture War in the Classroom

Nowhere are these culture-war issues more visible than in America's public schools. Some of the earliest battles over religious expression in the public arena—particularly Bible reading and prayer—were fought in the public schools during the 1960s and 1970s, losing big to the forces of secularism. Henceforth it might be possible to present the Bible as literature or history, but it would be illegal to treat Christian beliefs as real or true—rather like the "plastic reindeer test." Teachers could now give Jesus no more credibility than Zeus, Zoroaster, or Puff the Magic Dragon, and generations of young Americans would be conditioned to regard their Judeo-Christian heritage more as quaint custom or myth.

And still the battles continue. The following is a sampling from *WorldNetDaily*:[42]

- In Massachusetts, members of a Bible club wanted to pass out candy canes with an attached religious message, but were told by their school superintendent it would violate the rights of the recipients. When the students did it anyway, they were suspended, and it took a sixty-seven-page court ruling in their favor for school officials to back off.
- In Washington, a schoolgirl was not allowed to sing the word "Christmas" and instead was ordered to substitute "winter."
- In Florida, a school principal initially banned the name "Jesus Christ" on a Christmas party invitation poster.
- In Virginia, officials at a state school for the deaf and blind banned religious songs from a Christmas program.
- In Texas, in a report on volunteer work done for a squadron Christmas party, "Christmas" was crossed out and replaced with "holiday."
- In another Texas locale, students were told they could not wear red and green because those are Christmas colors.
- In Arizona, a public school choir director sought legal advice to have her choir perform Christmas carols.
- In New Jersey, a school banned some Christmas carols in a school program and replaced words in traditional pieces such as "Silent Night" with secular words.

- In Minnesota, a library's Christmas tree must be called "holiday" tree because it has become an "offense" to one worker due to its Christian meaning.
- And, among dozens of other cases, in Illinois an employer told a worker not to say, "Merry Christmas."

As we can see, what happened in April 2009 in the Georgetown Cover-up had actually been in the making for a long time. It took two hundred years since Jefferson's presidency (1801–1809) until it was possible for a U.S. president to be able tell Muslim leaders, with a straight face, that America is as much a Muslim nation as a Christian one. Or as candidate Obama put it, "Whatever we once were, we are no longer a Christian nation."

2.

THE GLOBAL AND LEGAL WAR ON CHRISTIANITY

> Even if we regard every high school student's decision to attend a home football game as purely voluntary, we are nevertheless persuaded that the delivery of a pregame prayer has the improper effect of coercing those present to participate in an act of religious worship.
>
> —*U.S. Supreme Court justice John Paul Stevens, writing the majority opinion in* Santa Fe Independent School District v. Doe, *which upheld a lower court's ban on voluntary student prayer before high school football games, June 19, 2000*

A POLL OF more than 10,000 likely voters conducted in March 2010 by Zogby International, and commissioned by *The O'Leary Report*, found that just 36 percent of American voters think states should pass legislation that recognizes same-sex marriage. Nearly 28 percent of voters would prefer that states adopt policies that recognize same-sex domestic partners for the purpose of receiving state-sanctioned benefits, and 29 percent want no legal recognition of same-sex unions whatsoever.

It's clear that somewhere along their journey to win equal rights, gay marriage proponents lost their way. In addition to these poll numbers that say so, it becomes more evident with each passing election cycle, when blue state voters turn out in droves to elect pro-gay marriage candidates, but vote against ballot initiatives that would sanction gay marriage.

For example, in 2008 a majority of voters in both California and Florida turned out to vote both for President Obama and against gay marriage. In all, thirty-one states have held voter referendums on whether or not to sanction gay marriage, and in all thirty-one instances gay marriage has lost.[1]

The cause of this seemingly schizophrenic voter backlash is the perception among Americans—both those who favor and oppose gay marriage—that the gay lobby isn't merely interested in legislating civil rights, but rather legislating acceptance of their lifestyle.

This mandate that everyone must view homosexual marriage as a societal norm is perfectly illustrated in a recent battle between the District of Columbia and the Catholic Church.

In December 2009, the D.C. City Council passed an ordinance that legalized gay marriage in the District. But that's not all. Private charities that provide social services within the District would be required to hire gay men and women, provide employee benefits to same-sex married couples, and allow them to adopt. The Catholic Church, which is one of the largest social service providers in D.C., rightly noted that such a mandate would violate its right to operate freely, under the First Amendment, in a manner that reflects the Church's values and principles.

When the Church told the Council that it may have to cease providing its services in D.C., Democratic council member Tommy Wells fumed: "It's a dangerous thing when the Catholic Church starts writing and determining the legislation and the laws of the District of Columbia."[2] This is the precise flawed logic that pushes so many voters into the anti–gay marriage camp. The Church isn't writing the law. The Church is saying that the law violates its beliefs, and as such, it can't operate within the law's structure. And given the choice, it would rather stay true to its belief system than scrap a core tenet of its faith because a few D.C. council members said so.

Susan Gibbs, a spokesperson for the Archdiocese of Washington, countered Mr. Wells' flawed logic nicely, explaining: "We are not threatening to walk out of the city. The city is the one saying, 'If you want to continue partnering with the city, then you cannot follow your faith teachings.'"[3] Indeed, the city council refused to add a religious exemption to its bill.

Opponents of gay marriage in the District tried to have the matter put to a voter referendum; however they were blocked by D.C. Judge Judith Macaluso, who, in a bout of judicial activism, ruled that D.C. voters would not be allowed to decide the matter for themselves. In particularly galling fashion, Judge Macaluso ignored precedent and grounded her ruling in the city's Human

Rights Act, saying that the Act forbids discrimination on the basis of sexual orientation. Never mind that in 1995, in the case of *Dean v. District of Columbia*, the D.C. Court of Appeals ruled that the city's Human Rights Act did *not* protect gay marriage, and was never "intended to change the ordinary meaning of the word 'marriage.'"[4]

As of this writing, it appears that the Catholic Archdiocese of Washington has three options, and none of them are attractive. It can stop providing benefits to any of its employees (i.e., if it doesn't provide benefits to married couples, it can't be accused of discriminating against same-sex couples), but that would mean harming its married employees. Its second option is to acquiesce to the demands of the D.C. Council, but that would mean essentially jettisoning a core tenet of its doctrine. Finally, the Church can stop helping poor families and children in the District of Columbia, but that would mean turning its back on people in need.

Gay marriage activists don't seem to realize that when they go beyond forcing their philosophy on others—to forcing actual behaviors on others as well—they end up driving voters away from their cause. Even some voters who might otherwise sympathize with their plight.

The War in Italy

Luigi Cascioli probably never heard of the "plastic reindeer test," but he would no doubt approve. This ex-priest, in his midseventies, from a town north of Rome, has been working the legal system there in an attempt to have Christianity declared a myth and the Catholic Church prosecuted for fraud. He began by filing suit against a local priest for asserting that Jesus Christ was a real person who lived two thousand years ago and violating Italian laws prohibiting "abuse of popular credulity" and "impersonation." A judge in Viterbo rejected those claims, which did not surprise Cascioli in this predominantly Catholic nation.[5] But he's not done. Cascioli has published a book, *La Favola di Cristo* (*The Fable of Christ*), allegedly disproving Christ's existence; maintains an active Web site promoting his views; and is pressing a legal case for "religious racism" against the Church through the European Court of Human Rights.[6]

The point is not so much what one person who abandoned his faith has accomplished (so far nothing tangible), but the direction Western society is going and the huge potential for ill that exists through crafty use of one of the pillars of Western democracy—the judiciary. Americans have become accustomed to endless legal battles instigated in U.S. courts by antireligion forces like the Freedom from Religion Foundation and ACLU over a tired list of pet issues—gay rights, hate crimes, separation of church and state, ad nauseam. But we're not alone. For a real exercise in déjà vu, just travel around Europe and see how many of the same issues are being replayed in scores of courtrooms and legislative chambers across the continent. And for starters, just look across the border.

The War in Canada

So-called human rights commissions have become a veritable plague on the body politic in Canada. These are quasilegal, extrajudicial bodies with a license to seek and destroy offensive speech and to turn the speaker's life into a living hell. Their potential downfall is the willingness of some individuals to embrace that kind of abuse for the sake of principle, such as strongly held religious beliefs. One such individual is Bill Whatcott, an evangelical Christian and licensed practical nurse in Saskatchewan who has publicly campaigned against abortion and homosexuality. For his efforts, Whatcott has been slapped with a "lifetime ban" on public criticism of homosexuality and been forced to pay $17,500 to four homosexuals he had offended.[7] He has also had his nursing license suspended, and has been fined $15,000 for his pro-life activities.

Whatcott has been arrested numerous times for violating the "bubble zone"—a sixty-foot no-protest setback—at abortion clinic entrances. Eventually, Whatcott's nursing license was reinstated by an appeals court that upheld his off-duty right of free speech. Yet, the message could hardly be clearer that free speech in Canada today comes at a very high price. Fortunately, there are quite a few Canadians sufficiently committed to principle to pay that price.

Another is Stephen Boissoin, a pastor who wrote a letter to the editor of his local newspaper, denouncing what he thinks is an unholy homosexual agenda.

"From kindergarten class on," Boissoin wrote, "our children, your grandchildren are being strategically targeted, psychologically abused and brainwashed by homosexual and pro-homosexual educators."[8] An activist professor at the University of Calgary filed a complaint of "hate-mongering" against Boissoin. The professor cited the case of a young homosexual who was beaten up two weeks later as evidence that such expressions incite violence. "Sexual orientation" was added to the protected categories under a federal hate crime law in 2004. Boissoin was fined $5,000 by the Alberta Human Rights Commission and ordered to "cease publishing in newspapers, by e-mail, on the radio, in public speeches, or on the Internet, in future, disparaging remarks about gays and homosexuals."[9] The case is on appeal over constitutional issues.

Similarly, the religious magazine *Catholic Insight* is under legal attack after a gay activist accused it of making "derogatory" remarks about homosexuals.[10]

Being "Islamophobic" in Canada can get you in about as much trouble as being "homophobic." Toronto Pastor Mark Harding objected when his local high school began handing out Qurans and making special accommodations for Muslim students to pray at school, while others were denied such privileges. Harding was prosecuted for "promoting hatred" against a religious group and sentenced to two years probation and 340 hours of community service under supervision of a Muslim imam. He was forced to undergo Islamic "re-education," including readings denigrating non-Muslims. A gag order restrained Harding from criticizing Islam or Muhammad or speaking about his case.[11]

The War in Britain

Britain's hate crimes laws have been updated to include "incitement to hatred of homosexuals," with penalties of up to seven years in prison—a longer sentence than the five years typically meted to a rapist. Reports of police intimidation consequently have been on the rise, especially for clergy whose sermons and statements stray into the area of sexual morality. Catholic archbishop Mario Conti of Glasgow, Scotland, for example, was reported to the police in 2006 for asserting in a sermon that civil partnerships undermine marriage. A Catholic journalist, Lynette Burrows, was interrogated by police after questioning the rights of gays to adopt children.

Ironically, the law is also affecting Muslims, an uber-protected religious class in Britain, but who also tend to hold dim views of homosexuality. Sir Iqbal Sacranie, head of the Muslim Council of Britain, was questioned by police after describing homosexuality as harmful in a radio interview. Neil Addison, a lawyer who has represented defendants in these cases, said, "Increasingly, hate-crime laws are being used to harass and intimidate ordinary people who dare to disagree with PC (politically correct) orthodoxy."[12]

As well as some extraordinary ones. In one infamous case, ultraconservative American radio talk show personality Michael Savage was denied entry to the U.K. because of his outspoken views on homosexuality.

What would you say if you were a teacher at a government training session and you were caught off-guard with the question, "What makes you think it's natural to be heterosexual?" Chances are, you would default to your religious beliefs, maybe even quote scripture. Of course, you'd be falling right into the trap.

Kwabean Peat, a Christian teacher in London, recognized the trap and decided to walk out with several other colleagues instead. He also wrote to three other staff members, complaining of the lesbian presenter's "aggressive" homosexual agenda. At least one of the staff members reported Peat, and he was suspended for "harassment" and "intimidation" and "gross misconduct."[13] At last report, Peat may be able to return to work if he stifles himself and agrees to talk no further about the incident.

Also contributing to this PC orthodoxy in the U.K. is a total lack of religious radio broadcasting. It's been banned there since 1990, placing England alongside Saudi Arabia, Afghanistan, and Iran in that distinction.

The War in Sweden

Scandinavia has a much-deserved reputation as the home of everything politically incorrect. But there are limits even there. It was a Danish newspaper, for example, that published the controversial "Muhammad cartoons," depicting the Prophet in a less-than-flattering manner and igniting a firestorm of protest from Muslims. Not even U.S. newspapers were willing to publish this material, adopting a form of intimidation-based self-censorship. And while homosexual civil unions are universal throughout Scandinavia, it was in Sweden where the forces of secularization-by-intimidation finally met their match. It was solely the work of one man, a small-town Pentecostal preacher whose conscience moved him to take a stand regardless of the cost.

Deliberately risking prosecution, Åke (pronounced *Oh-keh*) Green, pastor of a tiny church on a big island, preached a message on July 20, 2003, that may have changed the course of history. He cited sixteen passages of Scripture for God's view of homosexuality, which he termed "abnormal" and a "perversion." Green, sixty-three, was prosecuted and convicted of "incitement to hatred" and sentenced to a month in prison.[14] Green's appeal went all the way to Sweden's Supreme Court, which played his sermon in its entirety, and Swedish radio broadcast it to the entire nation. Green was acquitted after his attorney threatened to take the case to the European Court of Human Rights and cause additional international embarrassment. The Swedish government feared it could have been found in breach of free-speech provisions of the international Universal Declaration of Human Rights.

It is hard to overstate the significance of the Åke Green case. Emboldened by his example, other Swedish clergy began to find their voice. Eight hundred Swedish Lutheran priests signed an online petition rejecting mandates from their national church to officiate and bless same-sex partnerships. Per Karlsson, who heads the Swedish branch of Advocates International, a human rights-legal consortium, observed, "It was clearly a victory that Green was acquitted and that in Sweden a minister, citing Scripture, can speak out in opposition to homosexual behavior. This has now been carved out as safe territory."[15]

The war against religion and freedom of speech rages on in other nations as well.

The War in the Netherlands

Dutch Member of Parliament and leader of the conservative Freedom Party, Geert Wilders, is being prosecuted for hate crimes for his hard-hitting short film *Fitna*, which explores terrorism and radical Islam. He also has been denied entry to the United Kingdom as a dangerous person. Still, Wilders may be fortunate. Theo van Gogh, a descendant of the famous artist, was murdered in 2004 for producing a movie critical of Islam, and in 2002, Dutch politician Pim Fortuyn was murdered for his views on Islam and Muslim immigration.[16]

The War in Italy

Author Oriana Fallaci was prosecuted for "defaming Islam" when she wrote that Islam "brings hate instead of love and slavery instead of freedom." She died in September 2006, two months after the start of her trial.

The War in Australia

Pastors Daniel Scot and Danny Nalliah were prosecuted in 2004 for hate speech in violation of Australia's 2001 Racial and Religious Tolerance Act for statements that some Muslims called offensive. The Becket Fund for Religious Liberty, which assisted in the pastors' defense, said the effect of the "tolerance" act was to turn the country's courts into "sermon review boards."[17] As part of their punishment, the pastors would have been forced to make public apologies, but they said they would go to prison first.

In 2006, the Supreme Court of Victoria found in favor of Scot and Nalliah, sparing them from prison. Meanwhile, the country is considering adoption of a Canadian-style Human Rights Charter that family and pro-life advocates fear will further muzzle Christians.

U.S. Court Cases

Following are some recent U.S. cases raising significant issues for freedom of religious expression, according to legal sources noted in parentheses at the end of each summary.

Van Orden v. Perry and McCreary County, KY et al. v. ACLU

These two cases illustrate why Ten Commandments case law has a reputation for being "messy." Both were decided on the same day (June 27, 2005) by the U.S. Supreme Court, but with opposite verdicts. The Van Orden case was a constitutional challenge to a six-foot-high Ten Commandments monument between the Texas Capitol in Austin and the state Supreme Court building, the site of a number of monuments and historical markers. The high court ruled in favor of this monument, but against two others at Kentucky county courthouses (McCreary). The difference seemed to be the degree to which the Texas display appeared to have a secular historical purpose, which the Kentucky ones supposedly lacked. Both rulings were 5–4, with the sole difference being the swing vote of Justice David Breyer. (Rutherford Institute, Liberty Counsel)

Glassroth v. Moore

On August 1, 2001, Alabama Supreme Court Chief Justice Roy Moore had a 5,280-pound block of granite with the Ten Commandments engraved on it, installed at the State Judicial Building. A group of lawyers filed suits in federal court to have the monument removed as a violation of the Establishment Clause. The district court agreed and in November 2002 ordered Moore to remove the monument. The Court of Appeals affirmed the original decision in July 2003, then set a deadline in August for the monument's removal. When Moore failed to comply, the district simply ordered the building manager to remove it. Moore was later removed from office for judicial misconduct for failing to comply with the order of the federal court.[18]

Green v. Haskell County Board of Commissioners

In a suit brought by the ACLU, a federal appeals court ruled that a Ten Commandments monument at the Haskell County, Oklahoma courthouse endorses religion based on comments made by county commissioners when it was installed. After this ruling, County Commissioner Mitch Worsham had more words: "Whoever was the judge in this, I feel sorry for him on Judgment Day. We're not going to take it down."[19] Attorneys with the Alliance Defense Fund plan to appeal the case to the U.S. Supreme Court.

Meanwhile, the Oklahoma Legislature jumped into the fray by voting to erect a Ten Commandments monument on the State Capitol grounds identical to the one in Austin, Texas, that survived Supreme Court review. (Alliance Defense Fund, First Amendment Center)

Newdow v. United States Congress, Elk Grove Unified School District, et al.

The infamous Michael Newdow challenge to the words "under God" in the pledge of allegiance in Sacramento, California schools ended up being a lot of sound and fury signifying very little. Initially the Ninth U.S. Circuit Court of Appeals, the most overturned federal appeals court in America, teed up another big one for the Supreme Court by ruling against the schools and finding that "under God" was an unconstitutional government endorsement of religion. It ended not with a bang but a whimper when the high court skated around the main issue and threw the case out on a technicality—"standing." That is, the custodial parent of the child exposed to this language was not Michael Newdow, but his ex-wife. Therefore, he did not have standing to bring the lawsuit. (Rutherford Institute)

Marsh v. Chambers

In 1983, Ernest Chambers, a member of the Nebraska legislature, challenged the legislature's practice of having a chaplain employed by the state offer a prayer at the beginning of each legislative session. Lower courts supported Chambers, but the chaplaincy practice was upheld by the U.S. Supreme Court. In his written opinion, Chief Justice Warren Burger abandoned the three-part test that had been the standard for cases involving the Establishment Clause (*Lemon v. Kurtzman*), relying instead on historical custom. Prayers by tax-supported legislative chaplains could be traced to the First Continental Congress and to the First Congress that framed the Bill of Rights. So, the chaplaincy practice had become "part of the fabric of our society," and such prayers are not an establishment of religion.[20]

Adair v. England (Sec. of Navy)

Thirty-four Navy chaplains are suing the U.S. Navy for discrimination by allegedly giving preferential treatment to chaplains from Roman Catholic and "liturgical" Protestant traditions. This included promotions, use of on-post facilities, and performance ratings. The U.S. Supreme court has refused to hear the case, but parts of it are still in the federal courts. (Rutherford Institute)

Larsen v. England (Sec. of Navy)

Four evangelical ministers claim they were denied Navy commissions as chaplains because of their denominational affiliation. One allegedly was told he would be viewed as more qualified if he were a "baby baptizer," referring to mainline "liturgical" denominations. They also charge that the Navy operates an unconstitutional denominational quota system. The case is before the D.C. District Court. (Rutherford Institute)

Veitch v. Danzig

A minister of the Reformed Episcopal Church alleges he was forced to resign his commission as a Navy chaplain or face court-martial for refusing to stop preaching "divisive" evangelical doctrine. The case was dismissed by federal district court and is on appeal. (Rutherford Institute)

Good News Club v. Milford School District

Stephen and Darleen Fournier sought approval from the Milford, New York, public schools to host after-school activities of the Good News Club, a private Christian organization for children. Milford rejected the request, saying songs, Bible lessons, Scripture memorization, and prayer constituted "religious worship" prohibited by the community use policy. The Club filed suit, alleging that its free speech rights under the First and Fourteenth Amendments had been violated. Lower courts held that Milford's denial was Constitutional, and because the subject matter of the Club was "quintessentially religious," the district's action was not unconstitutional viewpoint discrimination.

The U.S. Supreme Court, however, overturned the lower courts in 2001 and ruled for the Good News Club. Justice Clarence Thomas wrote that, "Milford's restriction violates the Club's free speech rights and that no Establishment Clause concern justifies that violation. . . . When Milford denied the Good News Club access to the school's limited public forum on the ground that the Club was religious in nature, it discriminated against the Club because of its religious viewpoint in violation of the Free Speech Clause of the First Amendment."[21]

Horowitz v. County of Los Angeles

Under pressure from the ACLU, the Los Angeles Board of Supervisors voted in September 2004 to remove the cross from the county seal to avoid a perceived establishment of religion. The Individual Rights Foundation filed a complaint in Los Angeles County Superior Court to challenge this decision on the grounds that it reflected a hostility to religion, violated the federal and California Constitutions, and involved a waste of taxpayer funds. The case was ultimately dismissed based on the dismissal of an earlier federal case raising similar issues. (Individual Rights Foundation, Claremont Institute)

Turner v. the city council of the City of Fredericksburg, VA

Pastor and Fredericksburg City Councilman Hashmel Turner challenged a council policy that forbids sectarian references in opening prayers by council members. Turner's suit claimed that the policy violated his First Amendment right to invoke the name of Jesus in his prayers. A federal district court granted the city's motion to dismiss the complaint in August 2006, and the Rutherford Institute filed an appeal. Retired U.S. Supreme Court justice Sandra Day O'Connor, sitting by special appointment on the Fourth U.S. Circuit Court of Appeals, wrote a 2008 decision for a unanimous three-judge panel upholding the city's policy against invoking the name of Christ. The U.S. Supreme Court has refused to hear the case. (Rutherford Institute)

Kiesinger v. Mexico Academy

As part of a fund-raising campaign, Robert Kiesinger bought a brick for the walkway at Mexico Academy High

School (Oswego County, New York) and had it inscribed "Jesus Saves." School officials had this and other purchased bricks with Christian inscriptions removed from the walkway, even having some jackhammered to remove them. Any bricks with the name of Jesus were rejected as promoting a specific religion. This free speech and equal protection case is pending before a New York federal district court. (Rutherford Institute)

Rundus v. U.S. Department of Homeland Security

In 2006, Darrel Rundus' Christian ministry, Great News Network, had its offices raided by federal agents without a warrant. The agents confiscated every one of the ministry's "Million Dollar Bill" religious tracts, which were nothing but phony one-million-dollar bills with gospel tracts printed on them, as well as the text: "The million-dollar question: Will you go to Heaven?" The agents took the bills claiming violations of federal counterfeiting laws.

However, the bills are no different in appearance from numerous other fake currency that is frequently and openly sold and distributed in the United States Moreover, there is no such thing as a real one-million-dollar bill. The bills in question are produced by Ray Comfort and his Living Waters ministry as an evangelism tool, and an estimated 10 million of them have been distributed over the past ten years without any interference by the government. Rundus acquired the help of Liberty Counsel, which is suing Homeland Security for violating both his

First Amendment right to free speech and his Fourth Amendment guarantee against unlawful search and seizure. (Liberty Counsel)

Borden v. School District Township of East Brunswick, NJ

All Marcus Borden, football coach at East Brunswick High School, asked was the right to bow his head silently and "take a knee" with his players as they offered pre-game prayers. This had been part of the team's pregame routine for more than twenty-five years, but school officials forbade employee participation. A federal district court ruled that Borden was within his Constitutional rights to participate, but lost the next round when the school district and Americans United for Separation of Church and State appealed. Next stop, the U.S. Supreme Court. (Rutherford Institute)

Meeker v. Rockwell Collins Inc.

A Christian systems engineer was fired in 2008 after voicing a religious objection to his employer's diversity training initiative, which required that employees accept, celebrate, and embrace homosexuality. A suit filed in the U.S. District Court for the Northern District of Iowa on behalf of Thomas Meeker alleged that Rockwell Collins, Inc., in Cedar Rapids, Iowa, violated various state and federal laws when it refused to exempt Meeker from aspects of the company's diversity training that conflicted with his religious beliefs. Meeker, initially suspended, returned to work but informed his manager that he could not agree to participate in all required training. He was immediately ordered to leave the facility. A week later, Meeker received a letter from Rockwell Collins terminating his employment on the grounds that "We believe that you are unwilling to treat gay or lesbian co-workers with respect in the workplace." (Rutherford Institute)

Patrick v. State of Michigan Dept. of Treasury—Office of Financial Aid

Jordan Patrick received an unpleasant surprise when he decided to pursue a master's degree in pastoral studies at Cornerstone University. He was informed that this choice invalidated a tuition grant he had been qualified to receive from the state of Michigan. The state claimed the money could not be used toward a degree in divinity, theology, or religious instruction. (Rutherford Institute)

Carpenter v. District 10 School Board

Motivational speaker Jaroy Carpenter agreed to come to Dillon, Montana, at the invitation of a Christian youth organization to help students cope with a string of teen suicides and automobile deaths. The District 10 School Board initially agreed to have Carpenter, a former school teacher, address a middle school assembly in a nonreligious presentation on respect for self and others and making wise choices. After Carpenter's religious affiliations became an issue, the board rescinded its invitation. The case is pending before the Ninth U.S. Circuit Court of Appeals. (Rutherford Institute)

Dobrich v. Walls

Despite warnings from the ACLU, the Indian River School District (Delaware) Board of Education continued to have public prayers at its monthly meetings. On August 24, 2004, the board not only prayed (a member read a prayer given by George Washington during the Revolutionary War), but it initiated a policy to allow student-led prayer at commencement exercises. As threatened, the ACLU sued the board members in both their professional and personal capacities. The case is before the U.S. District Court, Delaware. (Rutherford Institute)

Harris by Bannon v. Boca Raton School District

When a teacher at Boca Raton (Florida) Community High School complained that a student-painted mural contained the words "God" and "Jesus," the principal ordered the students to paint over the offensive words. The students, members of the Fellowship of Christian Athletes club, said they had only been told they could not use inappropriate or profane language. Lawyers for the students say their free speech and equal protection rights have been violated, and they have asked the U.S. Supreme Court to hear the case. (Rutherford Institute)

Nampa Classical Academy v. Idaho Public Charter School Commission

All the Nampa Classical Academy, a charter school in Idaho, wanted to do was maintain a copy of the Bible to use as a resource in its classrooms. For doing so, the Idaho Public Charter School Commission threatened to revoke Nampa's charter—even though the Supreme Court has consistently held that Bibles in public schools are Constitutional, so long as they are studied objectively as an educational resource. The case is being litigated on Nampa's behalf by the Alliance Defense Fund. "Nampa Classical Academy is endeavoring to exercise its right to provide the best possible education for its students and has decided to include the Bible, along with dozens of other religious and secular writings, as resources in its curriculum to enrich instruction of literature, history, and culture, among other topics," Fund attorney David Cortman explains. "Schools have been doing this throughout American history." (Alliance Defense Fund)

Barr v. City of Sinton

The city of Sinton, Texas, passed an ordinance attempting to shut down two houses next to Pastor Rick Barr's church where nonviolent former prison inmates received religious instruction. A lawsuit challenging this action claims it violates the First and Fourteenth Amendments. (Rutherford Institute)

First Congregational Church of Hamilton v. Hamilton, MA

First Congregational Church of Hamilton, Massachu-setts, alleges that the city's Historic District Commission has repeatedly denied the church's requests for permis-sion to remove a shed and build a fellowship hall and education center in its place. Nor has the Commission responded to the church's requests for how to obtain per-mission. Ironically, the church was founded there in 1713 and predates the town itself. (Rutherford Institute)

Heartland Schools v. Illinois Department of Taxation

A Christian school is challenging an administrative deci-sion to deny tax-exempt status to part of its property that the county does not believe is being used for educational purposes. (Rutherford Institute)

Mast, et al. v. Central Michigan District Health Department

Six Old Order Amish farmers of Gladwin County, Michi-gan, claim in a federal lawsuit that they were denied reli-gious accommodation by the Central Michigan District Health Department when they were required to install modern septic and sewage disposal systems. Despite tests showing that an alternate method the farmers were will-ing to use met and exceeded sanitary code requirements, the health department still refused to grant them a variance.

Their attorneys claim this denial forces the Amish to abandon their "plain" ways—i.e., no electricity, telephones, and cars—and threatens their deeply held religious beliefs. (Rutherford Institute)

Washegesic v. Bloomingdale Public Schools (1994)

This dispute was over a portrait of Jesus Christ that had been hanging alone in the hallway of the Bloomingdale Secondary School for thirty years. Eric Pensinger, then a senior, brought suit to remove a copy of Warner Sallman's famous portrait, "Head of Christ," from a hallway outside the gymnasium and the principal's office of the Bloomingdale Secondary School. Bloomingdale is a small rural community near Kalamazoo, Michigan. A federal district judge held that the portrait violated the Establishment Clause and must be removed. The decision was upheld on appeal.[22]

Americans United for Separation of Church and State v. Elmbrook School District, WI

Americans United for Separation of Church and State filed a lawsuit in April 2009 in federal district court in Milwaukee against the Elmbrook School District, Wisconsin, on behalf of nine graduates. Since 2000, high schools in the district in Wisconsin have held their graduation ceremonies in the sanctuary of Elmbrook Church, which features a twenty-foot-tall cross above the dais. "Thus, when graduates receive their diplomas on the dais, they do so beneath the large cross, and, in order to watch the ceremony, graduates and their guests must continuously look at the cross for over two hours."[23] The lawsuit argued that this policy violates the Establishment Clause of the U.S. Constitution. The court denied a request to move the 2009 graduations of two high schools to a secular venue.

Santa Fe v. Doe (2000)

For years, an elected student "chaplain" at Santa Fe (Texas) High School delivered a Christian prayer before each home varsity football game. Two families filed suit under the Establishment Clause, and the District Court enjoined the Santa Fe Independent School District from following this policy. The district modified it to permit student-initiated and student-led prayer at games and student elections to determine whether invocations should be delivered and by whom. The District Court ordered a modification to permit only nonsectarian, non-proselytizing prayer. But the Court of Appeals held that even that modified policy was invalid, and the U.S. Supreme Court held that the student-led, student-initiated prayers did violate the Establishment Clause. The Court concluded that the football game prayers were public speech taking place on government property at government-sponsored school-related events. In dissent, Chief Justice William H. Rehnquist noted the "disturbing" tone of the Court's opinion that "bristle[d] with hostility to all things religious in public life."[24]

★ ★ ★

The inescapable irony surrounding the legal war against religion—taking place both here in America and across the globe—is that the ones claiming the mantle of freedom and tolerance are the ones doing the persecuting and the censoring. anti-religious activists seem to think that freedom of speech and expression only extends to the secular artist or the Atheist filmmaker—not the priest in the pulpit or the religious talk show host behind the microphone. But who is the real bigot? The evangelical Christian who seeks to spread the Word of God, or the secular humanist who wants to strip him of his most basic human rights?

3.

ACADEMIA & RELIGION

It is a sad day in America when school officials are criminally prosecuted for a prayer over a meal. The Founders believed that religion and morality are the twin pillars of the Republic. Judeo-Christianity was taught in public schools, because such teaching was the foundation of liberty. George Washington said that whoever undermines the twin pillars of religion and morality cannot be called a "Patriot." It is outrageous and an offense to the First Amendment to punish a school official for a simple prayer.

—*Mathew D. Staver, Founder of Liberty Counsel and Dean of Liberty University School of Law, commenting on the ACLU's prosecution of school employees in Florida who wished to offer a blessing before a meal*

IT'S NO SECRET that America's institutions of higher learning, by and large, have become uncomfortable and sometimes hostile places for Bible-believing Christians. The stories are legion of young people going off to secular universities and encountering professors who ridicule their faith, values, and beliefs.

But what about the religious institutions? Where are they today in this struggle for the soul of a generation? Sadly, too often they're just as intimidated by the larger culture. Again, President Obama's Georgetown Cover-up is instructive. It's a sore subject with Catholic League president Bill Donohue. Not one to pull a punch in most circumstances, he becomes especially indignant on that debacle:

> The cowardice of Georgetown to stand fast on principle tells us more than we need to know about what is going on there, but the bigger story is the audacity of the Obama administration to ask a religious school to neuter itself before the president speaks there. No bishop who might speak at the White House would ever request that a crucifix be displayed behind him. Moreover, the same church-and-state fanatics who go nuts every time a polling place is set up in the basement of a Catholic school have been noticeably silent over this incident.[1]

"Is the pope Catholic?" has been a way of saying that something is so obvious it goes without saying. But if the pope worked at Boston College, you might really have to ask. Professors at this private Jesuit college were outraged—nay, *shocked*—when their classrooms were invaded in February 2009 by objects that violated their sensibilities: crucifixes. One department chairman worried that the crucifixes could have "a negative effect on students" who might find the icons "divisive." Other professors talked about leaving for a more "welcoming" academic environment.[2]

There would certainly be much to choose from. The aforementioned College of William and Mary in Virginia comes to mind. Founded in 1693 "to the glory of Almighty God," William and Mary has been known as the "Alma Mater of a Nation" because of its illustrious alumni, including Thomas Jefferson, James Madison, and John Marshall. George Washington got his surveying license there and served as its chancellor during his presidency. It became a public institution within the Virginia university system in 1906. But it was 2006 when William and Mary finally managed to distance itself completely from its Anglican roots by removing a small cross from the historic Wren Chapel to make the *chapel* more "welcoming."

That's the very word that President Gene Nichol actually used to explain why the cross had to go: "In order to make the Wren Chapel less of a *faith-specific* space, and to make it more *welcoming* to students, faculty, staff and visitors of all faiths, the cross has been removed from the altar area"[3] (emphasis added).

Nichol was so welcoming to diverse viewpoints that he even later allowed a Sex Workers' Art Show to perform on campus, including prostitutes and a stripper. Just call it your tuition dollars at work. Thousands of students and alumni who thought this was all too much, however, started a petition drive demanding Nichol's ouster and began withholding their donations to the school. Finally, in February 2008, the government board of The College decided not to renew Nichol's contract. His three-year term was the shortest of any president in the institution's long history.

Selective Censorship

At the University of Virginia, even abject blasphemers apparently are welcome. You want to publish a cartoon depicting God talking dirty and smoking in bed after having sexual relations with Mary? No problem. In fact, just such a cartoon was deemed worthy of publishing in the student newspaper, the *Cavalier Daily*, in March 2008. Only after a national protest spearheaded by the American Family Association (AFA) did the newspaper remove the cartoon from its Web site.[4] It apologized (sort of) to anyone who might have been offended, but suggested that the subject matter and its treatment were still fair game.

At the same time, UVA sought to muzzle *Wide Awake Productions*, a campus Christian newspaper, by denying the paper the same funding resources that it routinely made available to secular campus newspapers. The paper filed suit, arguing that their right to free speech and free press had been violated. This case of blatant discrimination went all the way to the U.S. Supreme Court, and in a 5–4 ruling, the Court decided that UVA had indeed violated the First Amendment rights of the Christian newspaper.

It was no joke when a Christian student was cursed out by his professor in front of the entire class at Los

Angeles City College. Anti-Christian prejudice is now so pervasive in academia that maybe Professor John Matteson assumed it would be okay to call Jonathan Lopez a "fascist bastard" and refuse to give him a grade. Lopez was participating in a class assignment to give a six- to eight-minute speech on "any topic," and he addressed the issues of God and morality. He referred to the dictionary definition of marriage as being between a man and a woman and read a passage from the Bible on the issue. Matteson interrupted Lopez, refused to allow him to finish the speech, called him a "fascist bastard," and dismissed the class. Later he placed an evaluation form on Lopez's backpack without a grade, stating: "Ask God what your grade is."[5] Lopez also said the teacher threatened to have him expelled when he complained to higher-ups.

Professor Matteson then found himself the subject of a federal lawsuit for violating Lopez's free-speech rights. "Public institutions of higher learning cannot selectively censor Christian speech," said David French, a lawyer for the Alliance Defense Fund, which represented Lopez. "This student was speaking well within the confines of his professor's assignment when he was censored and ultimately threatened with expulsion."[6]

French has had some personal experience with viewpoint discrimination himself. He recalled his experience of applying for a teaching position at Cornell University. The interviewer asked him, "I note from your CV that you seem to be involved in religious right issues. Do you think that you can teach gay students?" When he asked what she meant, she answered, "Many of our gay students are activists, and I'm concerned that there may be conflict." French said it made him wonder "How many gay applicants at Cornell have been asked: 'Do you think you can teach Christian students?'"[7]

Meanwhile, L.A. City College—the largest community college system in the nation, with 135,000 students—may come to regret hiring professors like Matteson. French and Lopez took the opportunity of this legal action to challenge the college's sexual harassment policy, which bans all "offensive" remarks on campus. U.S. District Judge George F. King granted a preliminary injunction against enforcement of this code while the lawsuit proceeds, ruling that use of broad, subjective terms such as "hostile" and "offensive," unlawfully prevent students from exercising their First Amendment rights.

Some other recent examples of anti-Christian bias in academia:

Christian Legal Society

The University of California's Hastings College of Law pulled the plug on the campus chapter of the Christian Legal Society (CLS) in 2004 after it refused to open up its membership to non-Christians and homosexuals. The CLS argued in federal court that this policy "would force the chapter to allow persons who hold beliefs and engage in conduct contrary to the CLS Statement of Faith, which includes a prohibition on extramarital sex, to join as voting members and to run for officer positions. . . . CLS

argues that is a violation of the right of expressive association to force a religious student organization to accept officers and voting members who hold beliefs and engage in
conduct in opposition to the group's shared viewpoints,
thereby inhibiting the group's ability to define and express
its message."[8] CLS won a similar case in federal court in
2006 after being disenfranchised at Southern Illinois University (SIU). But the liberal Ninth U.S. Circuit Court of
Appeals upheld a ruling that Hastings had not violated the
society's constitutional rights, so the case is headed to the
U.S. Supreme Court.

University of Wisconsin

The University of Wisconsin–Madison defunded the
University of Wisconsin Roman Catholic Foundation in
2006, citing the Establishment Clause. The Knights of
Columbus, a Catholic service organization, was also
denied recognition on the same grounds, and the University of Wisconsin–Superior denied recognition to Inter-
Varsity Christian Fellowship on charges of religious
discrimination.[9] The Wisconsin Board of Regents ultimately changed its policies to allow religious student
groups to restrict their membership after the Alliance
Defense Fund sued on behalf of InterVarsity. Lawyers
pointed out that the University of Wisconsin was in the
same district where the Seventh U.S. Circuit Court of
Appeals had already ruled in favor of the Christian Legal
Society in the very similar SIU case.

Tufts Christian Fellowship

An InterVarsity affiliate at Tufts University, the Tufts Christian Fellowship (TCF), was briefly "de-recognized" and lost its student funding after a complaint of discrimination from a lesbian student. Julie Catalano, who claimed that homosexuality was a biblically accepted practice, alleged that she had been denied a leadership position with the TCF because of her sexual orientation. The TCF appealed the disaffiliation, and the Foundation for Individual Rights in Education (FIRE) organized a nationwide petition drive in support of the group. The university finally reversed itself and reinstated the TCF, avoiding a lawsuit. Thor Halvorssen, FIRE executive director, said, "We are delighted and relieved that the TCF does not have to seek shelter in catacombs beneath the Tufts campus."[10]

Christian Student Association

California State University at San Bernardino denied the Christian Student Association a charter because of the group's membership restrictions, including religious beliefs and sexual orientation. Traditional Values Coalition chairman and founder Reverend Louis Sheldon said:

> A student club of Muslims should not be forced to capitulate their belief system to accommodate Christians, Catholics, or Jews. Likewise, the local African-American club or Mexican-based *MeCha* organization should not be forced to accept someone of another

ethnicity. Surely an on-campus homosexual club would not want an evangelical Christian who opposes homosexuality as its member. The state should not be in the business of dictating which beliefs are acceptable, all under the injudicious guise of preventing "discrimination."[11]

Alpha Iota Omega

The status of Alpha Iota Omega, a Christian fraternity with an outreach to the Greek community, was revoked by University of North Carolina (Chapel Hill) officials because it refused to sign an agreement not to discriminate against anyone on account of religious affiliation. AIO contended that complying with this rule would compromise its status as a Christian fraternity and violated its First Amendment rights. U.S. District Court Judge Frank Bullock granted the fraternity an injunction, allowing it to restrict its membership. UNC later changed its policy to allow religious groups (within certain limits) to restrict their membership, and the suit was dismissed in 2006. Greg Lukianoff, FIRE's director of legal and public advocacy, urged the application of some common sense. "College Republicans . . . don't have to include Democrats in their group," he said. "It's a basic common sense, moral right."[12] Commented ADF Senior Counsel Jordan Lorence, "This is not like a ski club refusing to accept a minority student. Should a vegetarian club be required to grant membership and officer positions to meat-eaters?"[13]

State-sanctioned Speech

Speech codes have been a mainstay of the political-correctness movement that engulfed America's campuses years ago, transforming them from bastions of free speech into veritable soviets of state-sanctioned expression. And when it comes to alleged acts of "bias," don't count on having the right to face your accuser. At William and Mary's Bias Incident Reporting Web site, anyone can file a bias complaint against another for incidents related to "race, gender, sexual orientation, religion, or other protected conditions." And the kicker: it's anonymous.[14] It's hard to imagine what Jefferson or Madison would have thought of push-button prosecution at their alma mater today, but it's probably not the kind of thing they originally had in mind for young Americans.

The problem is not just with a handful of institutions like William and Mary. The Foundation for Individual Rights in Education reports that hundreds of major public and private universities routinely trash the First Amendment and violate their students' rights to free speech.

In a 2006 assessment of U.S. institutions of higher learning, FIRE found that more than 73 percent of public universities maintained unconstitutional speech codes, despite court rulings striking down similar policies, and that most private colleges routinely ignore the very speech rights explicitly promised for students. This disregard is so common that FIRE maintains a "Speech Code of the

Month" bad-guy listing. Its August 2009 poster child was Northern Illinois University (NIU), where "harassment" is defined as words and deeds that "annoy, alarm, abuse, embarrass, coerce, intimidate, or threaten another person."

FIRE said NIU's policy "fails miserably":

> While the university may legitimately prevent students from threatening and intimidating one another, it most certainly cannot prohibit students from annoying and embarrassing one another, even intentionally. In fact, satire and parody—which are entitled to particularly strong constitutional protection—are frequently profoundly embarrassing and annoying to their targets. This policy is representative of the prevailing culture on so many college campuses nowadays, in which there is a presumed "right not to be offended"—a "right" that undermines the whole notion of a university as a "marketplace of ideas" where students learn by exposure to a variety of different opinions expressed in a variety of different ways—including opinions and forms of expression that may be offensive.[15]

Another example is New York University, which prides itself on open discussion and free discourse: "Free inquiry, free expression, and free association are indispensable to the purpose of the University." Just don't be caught expressing anything that could be construed as insulting, teasing, mocking, degrading, ridiculing, inappropriate, demeaning, or hostile, even in jest. FIRE called NYU's code "deeply troubling":

> [H]ow is "open discussion and free discourse" possible when students face punishment for any speech perceived by another as insulting, degrading, or even merely inappropriate? There are many important conversations to be had on matters such as race, religion, and gender that will likely—in a truly open debate—lead to feelings of insult or hurt. Such conversations are precisely what the First Amendment— and promises of unfettered speech such as NYU's—exist to protect. . . . NYU students deserve far better than this.[16]

Room with a View-point Discrimination

Emily Brooker certainly deserved better from Missouri State University than what she got in 2006. It was bad enough being bullied to lobby for a cause that violated her Christian conscience, but then she was subjected to the nightmare of an academic inquisition and retaliatory discipline. Frank G. Kauffman, Emily's instructor in the school of social work, required her to write a letter to the Missouri Legislature pressing for homosexual adoption. When she refused, Kauffman charged her with a serious academic grievance that threatened her degree, and an ethics committee grilled her for more than two hours about her religion and her attitude toward gays and lesbians. "A person was forced to publicly state a position on a hot-button cultural issue to her own government that she disagrees with," said ADF's David French, who handled the case. "You can't get a more fundamental violation of the First Amendment than that."[17]

To his everlasting credit, University President Michael T. Nietzel blew several gaskets when he heard about this sorry affair—and then saw to it that justice was done. Discipline against Emily Brooker was halted. Her record was cleared, tuition and fees were waived, and she was given additional compensation. Kauffman was put on leave, but not simply as a scapegoat. Nietzel commissioned an inquiry and found out that the problem was much deeper than Kauffman, who was eventually brought back on staff. Kauffman may have been poisoned by a "toxic" environment in a department badly in need of a total overhaul. According to a report generated from the inquiry, "many students and faculty stated a fear of voicing differing opinions from the instructor or colleague. This was particularly true regarding spiritual and religious matters."[18]

Sometimes the only circuit breaker for people caught in these toxic environments is the power of negative publicity—and a good lawyer. Christina Popa found that out at the University of California–Los Angeles (UCLA) when she was told she could not give thanks to "my Lord and Savior Jesus Christ" in her graduation statement from the

Department of Molecular, Cell and Developmental Biology. Gordon Klingenschmitt, the former Navy chaplain who was punished for praying in Jesus' name, picked up on Christina's story, even posting a petition on his Web site to protest the university's position. "This is another example of the improper application of separation of church and state," Klingenschmitt said. "As a government school, UCLA cannot prohibit religious expression."[19]

On her Facebook page, Christina posted e-mail correspondence with her faculty adviser, who at one point threatened to allow none of her remarks at graduation. While Christina's case attracted little attention in the mainstream media, it caught fire in the blogosphere, which has truly come of age as a social force. So when lawyers from the Alliance Defense Fund contacted UCLA, the university immediately folded its hand and reversed course. Christina was able to have her statement read at graduation. Said ADF attorney Heather Gebelin Hacker:

> Christian students shouldn't be silenced when expressing their beliefs at public universities and are entitled to the same rights as all other students. . . . We are pleased that UCLA officials understand that denying religious liberty to students is a violation of the First Amendment, not a requirement of it. A personal statement at a graduation ceremony is exactly that—personal—and in no way signifies an endorsement of religion by the school.[20]

Luke Goodrich, legal counsel to the Becket Fund for Religious Liberty, agreed:

> Public universities don't get to censor student speech just because the speech is religious. That's called viewpoint discrimination, and it's unconstitutional. Let's hope that UCLA's biology department knows more about biology than it does about Constitutional law.[21]

Forced to Apologize for Her Beliefs

Erica Corder's high school diploma was held hostage at Lewis-Palmer High School, near Colorado Springs, Colorado, until she apologized to the community for giving thanks to Jesus Christ at her 2006 graduation. Fearing her remarks would never be approved for delivery, Erica, one of the fifteen valedictorians, simply deviated from her prepared thirty-second script to spring these words on the audience:

> We are all capable of standing firm and expressing our own beliefs, which is why I need to tell you about someone who loves you more than you could ever imagine. He died for you on a cross over 2,000 years ago, yet was resurrected and is living today in heaven. His name is Jesus Christ. If you don't already know him personally, I encourage you to find out more about the sacrifice he made for you so that you now have the opportunity to live in eternity with him.[22]

Erica Corder is receiving an education in anti-religious bias that money could never buy. Like Emily Brooker's, Erica's First Amendment rights have been violated. Although she lost the first round in U.S. District Court, Liberty Counsel has taken her case to the Tenth U.S. Circuit Court of Appeals. Said Liberty Counsel's Steve Crampton:

> Erica Corder should have received a medal for her courageous message. Instead, the dream of her graduation address turned into an ongoing nightmare. . . . [T]here is simply no legitimate pedagogical interest in the school's harsh treatment of Erica, simply for her sharing her faith. Forcing Erica to write an apology with which she did not agree is something you might expect in a totalitarian regime, but not in a free republic.[23]

Driving While Christian?

The long arm of this particular kind of totalitarianism is reaching down even into secondary schools and home-schooling. How? Higher education exerts substantial leverage over "lower" education through the curricula and textbooks it recognizes in college entrance requirements—and those it shuns. See where this is going? Yes, those shunned materials just happen to be *Christian* curricula and textbooks.

Consequently, students taught using textbooks from Bob Jones University Press and A Beka Books may have trouble getting admitted to any school of the University of California, which adopted a policy in 2007 that science, literature, and history textbooks from such publishers would not qualify for core admissions requirements because of their Christian perspectives.

UC had no problem accepting the textbook *Western Civilization: The Jewish Experience* and *Issues in African History*. But *Christianity's Influence on American History* was a no-no. More: *Feminine Roles in Literature*; *Gender, Sexuality, and Identity in Literature*; and *Literature of Dissent* were just fine. But *Christianity and Morality in American Literature* was not. Acceptable: *Intro to Buddhism*; *Introduction to Jewish Thought*; *Women's Studies & Feminism*; *Raza Studies*. Rejected: *Special Providence: American Government*.[24]

Lawyers for Advocates for Faith and Freedom vowed to appeal this case after a federal district judge upheld California's right to discriminate in textbooks. What's next? Charges of DWC—driving while Christian? Separate water fountains? Taxpayer-funded abortions? Oh, wait. We're already headed down that path.

One bright spot: there are more Erica Corders in America's secondary schools who are not afraid to force some of these issues. Who would have thought, for example, that the Lord's Prayer could become an act of civil disobedience? But that's what happened at the 2006 commencement in Russell Springs, Kentucky, where word got out that graduating senior Megan Chapman was planning to pray during the ceremony. The ACLU filed suit and won a court gag order prohibiting her from praying. But the whole thing backfired when in a bold act of defiance the entire senior class demonstrated their support for Megan—and disdain for the ACLU—by standing and reciting the Lord's Prayer before all three thousand people in the gymnasium. The local Sanhedrin probably figured they couldn't arrest an entire senior class. In this case, the ACLU may have won a legal battle, but the students won the clear public relations victory. And Megan and her sister were rewarded with full scholarships to Liberty University in Lynchburg, Tennessee.

Matthew D. Staver, founder of Liberty Counsel and dean of Liberty University School of Law, said the issue is simple and straightforward, "The key to graduation prayer is that schools may neither command nor prohibit voluntary prayer or religious viewpoints."[25]

The Alliance Defense Fund has issued some guidelines to gauge whether students may be victims of "anti-Christian bigotry."[26] The answer may be yes if the institution in question:

- dictates leadership standards, including requiring that leadership positions be open to students who don't believe in your group's mission;
- restricts where or when your group can meet or engage in expressive activities, but places no such limitations on other groups that, for instance, advocate radical feminism or abortion;

- enforces a speech code that limits you or your group's right to speak disapprovingly of extramarital sexual, homosexual, or other behaviors;
- restricts how or where your group can advertise, or censors the ads' content but places no such requirements on other student groups' ads;
- mandates "diversity training" that attempts to force you to affirm behavior or viewpoints that violate your faith or conscience;
- has one set of rules for Christian groups applying for access to the student fee funding pool and other rules for secular student organizations.

Government "Hostility"

Ever wonder how public schools that ban Christian extracurricular activities can, at the same time, have gay and lesbian clubs? Actually, they can't—not without violating the law. The U.S. Supreme Court determined in *West Side Community Schools v. Mergens* (1990), that Christian students have no less right to have Christian clubs at schools that permit other student-interest clubs:

> Bridget Mergens was a senior at Westside High School in Omaha, Nebraska. She asked her homeroom teacher, who was also the school's principal, for permission to start an after-school Christian club. Westside High already had about thirty clubs,

including a chess club and a scuba-diving club. The principal denied Bridget's request, telling her that a religious club would be illegal in a public school. The year before, in 1984, Congress had addressed this issue in the Equal Access Act, which required public schools to allow religious and political clubs if they let students form other kinds of student-interest clubs. When Bridget challenged the principal's decision, her lawsuit became the Supreme Court's test case for deciding whether the Equal Access Act was constitutional. . . .

The Supreme Court ruled in favor of Bridget. Allowing students to meet on campus to discuss religion after school did not amount to state sponsorship of religion. The Court said: "We think that secondary-school students are mature enough and are likely to understand that a school does not endorse or support student speech that it merely permits."

If a public school allows only clubs tied to the school curriculum—a French club related to French classes, for instance—it can exclude clubs that don't connect to its educational mission. But once a school allows student-interest clubs—such as a scuba-diving club, environmental club, or jazz club—it cannot exclude religious clubs, political clubs, gay-lesbian clubs, or other groups. If the club is religious in nature, however, the school must refrain from active involvement or sponsorship, so that it doesn't run afoul of the Establishment Clause, the Court said.[27]

In 2003, Education Secretary Rod Paige issued an important set of guidelines for religious expression in the public schools. When observed, these guidelines can help restore some balance and reason for Christian students in areas including free time, class assignments, clubs, advertising, teachers' role, and student speeches. One organization that periodically monitors these issues and reports on them is Koinonia House, which stated, "Schools and teachers, parents and students should discuss these guidelines and become familiar with the religious freedoms students have in the public schools."[28]

Some excerpts from those guidelines:

The Supreme Court has repeatedly held that the First Amendment requires public school officials to be neutral in their treatment of religion, showing neither favoritism toward nor hostility against religious expression such as prayer. . . . As the Court has explained in several cases, "There is a crucial difference between *government* speech endorsing religion, which the Establishment Clause forbids, and *private* speech endorsing religion, which the Free Speech and Free Exercise Clauses protect."

Although the Constitution forbids public school officials from directing or favoring prayer, students do not "shed their constitutional rights to freedom of speech or expression at the schoolhouse gate," and the Supreme Court has made clear that "private religious speech, far from being a First Amendment orphan, is as fully protected under the Free Speech Clause as secular private expression." Moreover, not all religious speech that takes place in the public schools or at school-sponsored events is governmental speech. . . .

As the Supreme Court has explained: "The proposition that schools do not endorse everything they fail to censor is not complicated," and the Constitution mandates neutrality rather than hostility toward privately initiated religious expression.[29]

Grace before Meals Outlawed

We knew it would come to this: a northern Florida public high school principal and athletic director have been forced to stand trial—including possible jail time—for a mealtime prayer, not even in the presence of students. Pace High School Principal Frank Lay and Athletic Director Robert Freeman found themselves facing charges in federal district court in Pensacola for violating the conditions of a settlement reached the year before with the American Civil Liberties Union barring employees from promoting prayer during school-sponsored events. At a meal for school employees and booster club members who had helped with a field house project, Lay, a deacon at a local Baptist church, asked Freeman to offer a blessing for the meal. For that, the two could be fined $5,000 each and sentenced to six months in jail.

Liberty Counsel's Matt Staver said the event occurred on school property but after school hours and the two men had no idea they might be breaking the law. "I have been defending religious freedom issues for twenty-two years, and I've never had to defend somebody who has been charged criminally for praying," he said.

According to the *Washington Times,* the school district also agreed to forbid senior class president Mary Allen from speaking at graduation "on the chance that the young woman, a known Christian, might say something religious"—the first student body president in thirty-three years not allowed to speak.[30] Fortunately, Mary's fellow classmates rose to the occasion.

The prosecution of Lay and Freeman and the muzzling of Mary Allen provoked a response in the student body remarkably similar to what happened in Russell Springs, Kentucky. At their commencement exercise on May 30, 2009, many of the more than three hundred graduating seniors taped crosses to their mortarboards and stood for a defiant recitation of the Lord's Prayer. It's enough to inspire at least some hope for the future of the Founders' republic.

President Abraham Lincoln probably would shudder to see how his own words are playing out in our day: "The philosophy of the school room in one generation will be the philosophy of government in the next." Ironically, the same liberal reformers who are trying to remove religion from America's public square would never admit it, but what they're actually setting up in its place is another state-sponsored religion. Ken Connor, chairman of the Center for a Just Society, describes that replacement this way:

> Too many teachers today enter the classroom with an agenda far more ambitious than the simple desire to instill a love of learning; these teachers go into the education business to proselytize a religion. This religion is comprehensive in its scope. It will not tolerate dissent because it cannot withstand scrutiny. Ironically, the State is its staunchest advocate and most ardent defender.
>
> This state-sponsored religion teaches the theory of evolution as an indisputable fact, singling out and eliminating from its ranks proponents of intelligent design theory—or, heaven forbid, actual Creationists—with Puritanical zeal. This religion mandates the normalization of lesbian, gay, bisexual, and transgendered lifestyles with no regard for parental consent while singling out traditionalists as ignorant bigots in need of reprogramming. Thus the classroom, once a forum for critical thought, analysis, and debate that allowed for many competing points of view, is now used to transform raw human material into homogenous batches of progressive, enlightened, politically correct, intellectually timid, and spiritually vacant progeny, ready to shape tomorrow's world.

We must make our stand now before this new religion amasses so many converts that we find ourselves outnumbered, outmaneuvered, and ultimately, irrelevant.[31]

What is left to say but, "Amen!"

4.

THE HOLLYWOOD WAR ON CHRISTIANITY

Religion is detrimental to the progress of society.
—Bill Maher in his antireligious film, Religulous

THE GREAT CHRISTIAN thinker Francis Schaeffer figured out more than forty years ago how new ideas were born and propagated in the culture. They weren't suddenly arriving full-blown out of thin air; they followed a downward stair-step process: Philosophy → Art → Music → General Culture → Theology.[1]

Think of the Green movement, for example. Once upon a time, some intellectuals began talking and writing about the physical world in a new way, as if planet Earth itself were a living, breathing organism. This philosophy became known as ecology and environmentalism. A little later, artists and musicians began to adopt this philosophy as their own, and, through their influence, it became common knowledge to the rest of us. Eventually, there were radical Green parties in Europe and even a Green theology for Christians, sometimes known as Creation Care.

This became fractious within Christendom, however, as some leaders (notably the National Association of Evangelicals) tried to deliver their grassroots constituents to the global warming lobby. The move was recognized by many as an attempt by some evangelical leaders to curry favor with deep-pocketed liberal grant-makers.

What Schaeffer did not foresee was how the multimedia explosion—especially the proliferation of "new media" and the Internet—would take this dynamic to a whole new level. It's been a kind of decentralization in which anyone with the cyber-megaphone of a weblog (blog) can jump entire steps in the chain and potentially start a new idea or social movement from right within the general culture. It's a brave new world in which young minds trapped inside this pop-culture echo chamber routinely get most news and information from Jon Stewart (Comedy Central) and late-night TV talk show hosts. It's a popular culture in which three times more Americans can name a judge for *American Idol* than can name the U.S. chief justice.[2] And it's a culture in which "irreverent" is actually a compliment.

Schaeffer, however, definitely would have understood the ideological lockstep of these voices as no coincidence and how something like Bush Derangement Syndrome—an irrational, knee-jerk hatred of the Bible-believing forty-third president—could mimic a contagious disease. (Those interested in pursuing this concept further will find value in Malcolm Gladwell's *The Tipping Point: How Little Things Can Make a Big Difference* (Boston:

Little Brown, 2000). It became an equal-opportunity culture in which really bad ideas also could spread like a plague.

Ideological Lockstep

The important point is that there *is* an ideological lockstep—and it's anything but benign, orthodox family and religious values. Nowhere is this more clear than in the open sewer that flows out of Hollywood—which no longer invades just a few movie theaters in town, but now virtually every big-screen home TV in America.

Perhaps King Solomon had it right three thousand years ago: "Righteousness exalts a nation, but sin is a disgrace to any people" (Proverbs 14:34 NIV). As a society, we're reaping a lot of disgrace on Hollywood's account. College student Sam Stephenson, nineteen, of Colorado Springs, goes to Afghanistan as part of a church short-term mission trip and learns that most Afghans, contrary to stereotype, are not bomb-throwing terrorists. But he also learns that Afghans have a stereotype of their own of Americans—as drunks and sex addicts.[3] Such stories are legion. And how do these people get those ideas? Not from the emissaries, ambassadors, missionaries, or even soldiers—but from Hollywood, of course.

The natural tendency is to say, "They're doing it for the almighty dollar." But while these studios and their producers certainly are doing well enough, they may not be doing as well as they could if they produced more wholesome entertainment. This has been well documented.

The Christian Film & Television ministry, for example, analyzed the content and box office averages of more than 750 movies in 2004, 2003, and 2002. "Movies with strong moral messages, whether they were rated G, PG, PG-13, or R, consistently earn four to seven times as much money on average as movies with immoral messages, according to our biblical standards," said Dr. Ted Baehr, chairman and founder of the Commission.[4]

There's just no room for serious doubt—in addition to being cash-driven, Hollywood is ideology-driven. This is an industry that produced an atrocity like the blasphemous *Last Temptation of Christ* yet froze out a production that, when independently produced, turned out to be a box-office smash, *The Passion of the Christ*.

Last Temptation

The Last Temptation of Christ started life as a book published in 1955 by Nikos Kazantzakis, the author of another novel made into a famous movie, *Zorba the Greek*. *The Last Temptation* took such dark and obscene liberties with the life of Christ that the Catholic Church banned the book and the Greek Orthodox Church excommunicated Kazantzakis. When he died in 1957 from leukemia, he was buried in the city wall of Heraklion because the Orthodox Church would not permit burial in a cemetery.

Earlier that same year, Kazantzakis missed receiving the Nobel Prize for Literature by one vote. French existentialist Albert Camus, who won the prize, reportedly said his fellow leftist Kazantzakis deserved it "a hundred times more" than did he.[5]

In Kazantzakis's twisted version of the Gospel story, a flawed, confused Jesus uses his carpentry skills to construct Roman crosses for crucifying Jewish criminals. He tells his disciple Matthew that the Gospel he is writing is wholly inaccurate. He voyeuristically watches the prostitute Mary Magdalene have sex with a succession of ten men. He kisses other men on the lips. He laments his many sins. He begs the noble and reluctant Judas to end his agony by turning him in to the Romans. On the cross, he has a fantasy of escaping death to live a normal life. He imagines himself marrying—and making love to—first Mary Magdalene and then, after she dies, Mary and Martha, with whom he has children. He tries unsuccessfully to persuade the apostle Paul to stop preaching a crucified and resurrected Christ. Then he begs God to let him back on the cross and fulfill his purpose.

While that's shocking enough, the 1988 Martin Scorsese MCA/Universal film by the same name compounded the offense by creating full-color, big-screen images of these scenarios. The production provoked an unprecedented firestorm of Christian protest. At one point, a crowd of 25,000 protesters demonstrated outside Universal's Los Angeles headquarters. Hundreds of Christian radio stations joined the protest. Major Christian organizations, including the American Family Association and Campus Crusade for Christ, appealed for the movie to be withheld, even offering to buy it from the studio. In the face of all this popular angst, several thousand movie theaters declined to show *The Last Temptation*. Universal, however, responded with an open letter in newspapers across the country, saying that acquiescence to these forces would infringe on the First Amendment rights of all Americans.[6]

The protests may have hurt the film at the box office, but it earned Scorsese an Academy Award nomination for Best Director. The American Film Institute honored Scorsese with the Life Achievement Award, considered the highest career honor in Hollywood. The Peter Gabriel soundtrack won a Grammy in 1990 for Best New Age Album. The *New York Times* ran a full-page ad of raves:

> Martin Scorsese, America's most gifted, most daring moviemaker, may have created his masterpiece. . . . Highest rating, an extraordinary accomplishment. The Crucifixion is the strongest such scene of all time, and may be the movie scene of the year. . . . The most impressive biblical movie epic ever. Visually breathtaking and intellectually scorching . . . an extraordinary feat of filmmaking.[7]

Film critic and radio talk show host Michael Medved (who is Jewish) wrote that he found viewing *The Last Temptation* "as uplifting and rewarding as two hours and forty-four minutes in the dentist's chair."[8] In his classic, *Hollywood vs. America*, Medved tells of fellow critics who privately despised this "breathtakingly bad" movie while publicly praising it—because they didn't want to be on the same side as people like Reverend Jerry Falwell. Jack Valenti, president of the Motion Picture Association of America, claimed it was simply an American issue of free choice not to be dictated to by self-appointed censors. But there was more to it than that. Medved wrote:

> Would Mr. Valenti have spoken out in behalf of a film biography of slain black leader Malcolm X that portrayed him as a paid agent of J. Edgar Hoover's FBI who secretly worked to discredit the civil rights movement? What about a movie version of the life of the assassinated gay hero, San Francisco supervisor Harvey Milk, that suggested that he was actually a closet heterosexual (and inveterate womanizer) who only pretended to be gay in order to seek political advantage? Or a revisionist view of Holocaust victim Anne Frank that portrayed her as an out-of-control teenage nymphomaniac who risked capture by the Nazis night after night to satisfy her raging hormones?
>
> It is difficult to imagine the industry's leaders rallying to the support of any such outrageous and patently offensive projects in the way they rallied to the support of *The Last Temptation*. For Hollywood, in other words, some martyrs are more sacrosanct than others.[9]

A decade and a half later, Mel Gibson, the staunch but troubled Roman Catholic Academy Award–winning actor/director, found no takers in Hollywood studios for his film project on the last twelve hours of Jesus' life, *The Passion of the Christ.* So he financed it with $25 million of his own money. Gibson's film turned out to be a terrific return on investment, grossing $370 million at the box office. Compare that with the $7 million *The Last Temptation* made. Even when we adjust the Gibson film's gross receipts for inflation, it crushes *The Last Temptation* $245 million to $7 million.

Da Vinci Code

To see where this is all going, consider Dan Brown's 2003 novel, *The Da Vinci Code,* which was made into a 2006 film of the same name. Noted Christian author and scholar Dr. Albert Mohler said, "If you thought *The Last Temptation of Christ* was explosive, *The Da Vinci Code* is thermonuclear."[10] Specifically:

> The book claims that Jesus Christ was married to Mary Magdalene, that a child was born of this marriage, and that Mary and her child fled after the crucifixion to Gaul, where they established the Merovingian line of European royalty. Art historians may quibble with Dan Brown's details, and mathematicians may take issue with his summary of the Fibonacci Sequence, but as a theologian, my problem is the author's toying with such an easily dismissed heresy. Brown has

crossed the line between a suspense novel and a book promoting a barely hidden agenda, to attack the Christian church and the Gospel.[11]

Indeed, U.S. Catholic bishops rated the film "morally offensive" and condemned the depiction of the Jesus–Mary Magdalene relationship as "deeply abhorrent." The film also made fantastic claims about a massive conspiracy perpetrated for centuries by the secretive Opus Dei to conceal the truth about Jesus and the supposed fabrications in the Gospels. This ultraconservative sect of Catholicism was depicted as warped and vicious. A leading cardinal, Nigerian-born Francis Arinze, warned there were limits to what the church could continue to tolerate:

> Christians must not just sit back and say it is enough for us to forgive and to forget. Sometimes it is our duty to do something practical. . . . Those who blaspheme Christ and get away with it are exploiting the Christian readiness to forgive and to love even those who insult us. There are some other religions which if you insult their founder they will not be just talking.[12]

Columbia Pictures stuck to its guns and declined the church's requests to soften the attack, and was rewarded with box office receipts totaling $217 million.[13] Producers know they have nothing to fear from a pope issuing a *fatwa* against them or Catholic *mujahidin* declaring *jihad* against them. To show real courage, Universal and Columbia should consider producing something along the lines of a *Satanic Verses* by Salman Rushdie, the Iranian author who ended up with a price on his head for writing this book. It involved the legend that Muhammad's first draft of the Quran contained a nod to Arabian polytheism by naming the pagan goddesses Allat, al-Uzza, and Manat as daughters of Allah. Supposedly the prophet Muhammad had second thoughts and redacted those references, attributing them to the influence of Satan. If Universal and Columbia want to demonstrate that they are not meaning to bash Christianity, and merely standing on First Amendment courage, they should consider making *that* movie.

Al Mohler points out something significant here: Dan Brown didn't come up with these wacky ideas all on his own. Most of them were concocted by British authors Michael Baigent, Richard Leigh, and Henry Lincoln in their 1982 book *The Holy Blood, Holy Grail*, which in turn was based on forged documents from older French sources. The verdict of legitimate historians and scholars: Unadulterated poppycock.[14] For that matter, it would appear that Nikos Kazantzakis was tapping into this same poppycock. Both his and Brown's stories incorporate the legends of Jesus and Mary Magdalene moving to France, where their progeny gave rise to one of the royal families of Europe. This is probably not a coincidence.

Mockers and Scoffers

Remember Francis Schaeffer's stair-step process of cultural influence: Philosophy → Art → Music → General Culture → Theology. Widespread doubt has been sown throughout the general culture as to the veracity of Scripture and the validity of the church. This is huge, as the average person no longer feels it necessary to answer for his personal conduct or moral values. It's the church that's now on the defensive.

An unfortunate reality today is that the consumer-driven church is becoming increasingly hostage to the dictates of the general culture. Moral authority in the pastorate is succumbing to parishioners who vote with their feet. If Schaeffer was correct, it may be only a matter of time before the church starts to adjust its theology to accommodate this reality. Most likely it will come in the form of ever fewer pastors, priests, and preachers willing to stick their necks out to espouse the literal interpretation of inerrant Scripture—or worse, perhaps wholesale acquiescence to outright heresy. Some argue that this is already happening with the very postmodern Emergent Church movement.[15]

And, of course, this downward stair-step does not derive from just an occasional movie every few years. We now have similar influences daily in the mainstream media and on cable television from the likes of Bill Maher and

Comedy Central. Bill Maher, host of HBO's *Real Time with Bill Maher*, likened Christianity to a "neurological disorder." Maher told MSNBC's Joe Scarborough (*Scarborough Country*) that he was "embarrassed" that America was more like fundamental Islamic regimes because of the widespread belief in religious "fairy tales":

> We are a nation that is unenlightened because of religion. I do believe that. I think that religion stops people from thinking. I think it justifies crazies. I think flying planes into a building was a faith-based initiative. I think religion is a neurological disorder. . . . I don't hate America. I love America. I am just embarrassed that it has been taken over by people like evangelicals, by people who do not believe in science and rationality. It is the 21st century. And I will tell you, my friend. The future does not belong to the evangelicals. The future does not belong to religion.[16]

When Rosie O'Donnell was co-host of ABC's *The View*, she could be counted on for periodic eruptions such as, "Radical Christianity is just as threatening as radical Islam in a country like America." O'Donnell also blurted out, "If men could get pregnant, abortion would be a sacrament."[17] After the U.S. Supreme Court ruled that a federal ban on partial birth abortion (a procedure in which a viable baby is partly delivered and then slaughtered) was constitutional, O'Donnell declared the ruling "frightening" and then smeared the five Catholic justices on the Court as theocrats: "You know what concerns me? How many Supreme Court judges are Catholics? Five. How about separation of church and state in America?"

Rosie had no issue, of course, with Catholic Sonia Sotomayor's appointment to the high court. In fact, there wasn't nearly the volume of Catholo-phobia with liberal Sotomayor as there was with Catholics John Roberts and Samuel Alito before her. There were no media elites fretting about whether her religion might cloud her judgment, as they did with Roberts and Alito. The *Los Angeles Times*, for example, cited the "strong anti-abortion views" of Roberts's wife, whom it termed a "very devout Catholic."[18] It clearly was not meant as a compliment.

Hollywood Out of Step with Most Americans

You may find it heartening to know that a strong majority of Americans recognize Hollywood's anti-Christian bent, even if they do continue to flock to theaters nationwide to absorb it. A poll conducted in 2008 by the Marttila Communications Group found that 59 percent of Americans believe that Christian values are under attack in this country, and 59 percent say that "the people who run the TV networks and the major movie studios do not share the religious and moral values of most Americans." Sixty-three percent say that religion, as a whole, is losing its influence on American life, and a surprising 48 percent of Americans believe there is an "*organized campaign* by

Hollywood and the national media to weaken the influence of religious values in this country"[19] (emphasis added).

Christian film director Scott Derrickson, whose movie credits include *The Exorcism of Emily Rose* and *The Day the Earth Stood Still* notes that Catholics in particular get a raw deal from Hollywood. Catholics, says Derrickson, are often portrayed as sexually repressed killjoys, corrupt moneygrubbers, maddening hypocrites, fanatical criminals, medieval moralists, and predatory child rapists." Some examples he cites are the immoral Cardinal Glick in *Dogma* (played by George Carlin), the crazy Catholic mother in *The Others* (played by Nicole Kidman) and wicked Bishop Lilliman in *V for Vendetta* (played by John Standing).

"Most films and television shows try to balance out the portrayal of a Muslim extremist with the representation of reasonable Muslims or at least reasonable Arabs," Derrickson says. "Often that kind of concern for balance doesn't apply to Catholic representation. Showing a corrupt priest doesn't demand any counter-balancing representation."[20]

There is no need for counterbalance or sensitivity training when the object of your scorn is—as author Phillip Jenkins describes it—"the last acceptable prejudice" in America.

5.

THE MEDIA WAR ON CHRISTIANITY

> The group in this country that most resembles the Taliban, ironically, is the religious right.
>
> —*MSNBC political commentator Chris Matthews*

IF YOU'RE ONE of the nearly 70 percent of Americans who think the mainstream media is out of touch, it's likely because those talking heads and desk jockey reporters simply don't share your values and beliefs.[1] No matter how much effort journalists exert to repress their personal feelings, the fact is, those personal feelings almost always affect either how they report the news, or what news they choose to report. We all view the world through our own perspective. Journalists, as it turns out, have a perspective that is different from most Americans.

Roughly 42 percent of Americans attend church weekly or almost every week.[2] On the other hand, only 8 percent of national print and broadcast journalists say they attend church weekly, and only 9 percent say they worship almost every week.[3] An even larger values gap between the press and the people exists on the question of God and morality. A strong 58 percent majority of Americans say that belief in God is necessary to be moral. Only 6 percent of the national news media share this same belief.[4]

Christian "Persecution Complex"

After legendary CBS newsman Walter Cronkite died in July 2009, *Time* magazine conducted a poll asking who was now America's most trusted newscaster. The results: CBS's Katie Couric, 7 percent. ABC's Charlie Gibson, 19 percent. NBC's Brian Williams, 29 percent. Comedy Central's Jon Stewart, 44 percent.[5]

Yes, that Jon Stewart of Comedy Central's *The Daily Show* fame. The same Jon Stewart that likes to mock Christians like Bush Attorney General John "Mister Christian" Ashcroft and 2008 Republican Vice Presidential Nominee Sarah Palin.

During Ashcroft's Senate confirmation process, Stewart intoned, "Let it be done, in the name of the Father"—picture of President George H. W. Bush—"and the Son"—picture of President George W. Bush—"and the Holy Ghost"—picture of octogenarian Sen. Strom Thurmond. Stewart said Ashcroft's confirmation was all but assured because of the support of eleven Democratic senators delivered by "a key Ashcroft ally"—picture of Jesus at the Last Supper. "That'd be *Jesus* right there," he deadpanned when the audience appeared not to recognize the figure at the head of the table.[6]

And then sometimes Stewart can be as direct as the best of them. Speaking at homecoming festivities for Northeastern University in Boston, Stewart said, "I'd just like to say to Sarah Palin, 'F--- you!'"

The Alaskan governor and outspoken Christian was a regular butt of Stewart's mocking. Stewart—who identifies himself as a socialist—also likes to mock those who try to point out that there's an anti-Christian culture war going on: "Does anyone know . . . does the *Christian persecution complex* have an expiration date? Because . . . uh . . . you've all been in charge pretty much since . . . uh . . . what was that guy's name? Constantine. He converted in—what was it—312 A.D.? I'm just saying, enjoy your success"[7] (emphasis added).

Don Feder, president of Jews Against Anti-Christian Defamation, has a very different perspective on this Christian-bashing by liberals in the mainstream media:

> They've depicted the followers of Jesus—evangelical Protestants and traditional Catholics in particular—as superstitious degenerates, bigots, trailer-park misogynists, both sexually repressed and hypocritically lecherous, and a gang of Torquemada [Spanish Inquisition] wannabes who constitute a clear and present danger to democracy and the 21st century. . . . They've derided their values, indoctrinated their children, given their teenaged sons condoms (and told their teenaged

daughters how to get an abortion without their parents' knowledge or consent), used their tax dollars to fund "art" like a crucifix submerged in a jar of urine, eliminated the mildest public expressions of faith, and tried to overturn 3,300 years of Judeo-Christian tradition by mandating gay marriage from the bench. . . . [*Washington Post*] Reporter Michael Weisskopf contemptuously characterized conservative Christians as, "poor, uneducated and easy to command." This is an ugly stereotype, akin to saying that poor, ignorant darkies like to tap-dance while eating fried chicken.[8]

"Post-Christian" America

Young people may love Stewart's edgy irreverence, but evidently, most Americans don't buy the "Christian persecution complex" canard. A poll by a non-Christian organization found that most Americans do believe that there is a war against religious values. Recall the 2008 poll mentioned in the previous chapter that shows 61 percent of Americans believe religious values are under attack in our nation, 59 percent think TV networks don't share their religious and values, and 43 percent think the national media is deliberately trying to weaken the influence of religion on our country.[9]

The trend lines are also disturbing. "Christians are now making up a declining percentage of the American population," according to a *Newsweek* poll.[10] While the number of Americans who claim no religious affiliation has nearly doubled since 1990 (from 8 to 15 percent), according to *Newsweek*, the number of people willing to describe themselves as atheist or agnostic has nearly quadrupled in the same period (from 1 million to 3.6 million).

Al Mohler, president of the Southern Baptist Southern Seminary (Louisville), was disturbed by the findings, especially the shift to the Northeast as the new stronghold of the religiously disaffiliated. "That really hit me hard," he told *Newsweek* editor Jon Meacham. "The Northwest was never as religious, never as congregationalized, as the Northeast, which was the foundation, the home base, of American religion. To lose New England struck me as momentous." Mohler wrote in an online column:

> A remarkable culture-shift has taken place around us. The most basic contours of American culture have been radically altered. The so-called Judeo-Christian consensus of the last millennium has given way to a post-modern, post-Christian, post-Western cultural crisis, which threatens the very heart of our culture. . . . The evidence is overwhelming. Moral relativism has so shaped the culture that the vast majority of Americans now see themselves as their own moral arbiter. Truth has been internalized, privatized, and subjectivized. Absolute or objective truth is denied outright. Research indicates that

> most Americans believe that truth is internal and
> relative. No one, the culture shouts, has a right to
> impose truth, morality, or cultural standards. . . . In
> candor, we must admit that the Church has been
> displaced. . . . The old order is shattered, the new
> order is upon us.[11]

Let's examine some of the leading reasons given by the alienated: the church is too "anti-homosexual," "hypocritical," "judgmental," and "too involved in politics."[12] Does any of this sound familiar? Chances are you've recently heard the same verdict from a talking head or read the same message in your newspaper. And there is a definite age correlation as well. Those self-identifying as non-Christian comprise 23 percent of those over age 60; 27 percent for those 42–60; and *40 percent* of those 16–29. So, barring unforeseen developments, Bill Maher's assertion that "the future does not belong to religion" begins to look uncomfortably prophetic.

The "Smell of Death"

Two caveats: First, it's less than clear what is cause and what is effect here. Note *Newsweek*'s phraseology, "people *willing to describe themselves* as atheist or agnostic." Maybe it's not so much a growth spurt in the ranks of nonbelievers as a greater willingness to self-identify as such in a culture that no longer stigmatizes them as it once did—in fact, a culture that's trying hard to transfer the stigma in the other direction. The Bill Mahers and Jon Stewarts certainly have contributed to that process. Note, too, the recent rash of books by "New Atheism" authors like Christopher Hitchens (*God Is Not Great: How Religion Poisons Everything*), Richard Dawkins (*The God Delusion*), and Sam Harris (*The End of Faith: Religion, Terror, and the Future of Reason*). Maybe the only thing really new about the New Atheism is its marketability and general acceptance within our culture.

The second caveat is these objections of the religiously disaffected beg to be taken with a healthy grain of salt. "Hypocrisy"? That's not a reason; it's a rationalization— and a lame one at that. Try telling the judge that you don't obey speed limits because those signs have been put up by speeders. "Anti-homosexual"? "Too involved in politics"? "Judgmental"? These sound less like reasons not to believe than simply a desire for Christians to just shut the heck up. That's nothing new. The apostle Paul wrote about the same thing a couple thousand years ago: To those who are being saved, Christians are the "fragrance of life." To those who are perishing, they are the "smell of death."[13] In other words, don't fall for the idea that there's any kinder, gentler face that's going to fix this problem. The offense is largely in the eye (or nose) of the beholder.

"Offensive" Christians

CNN founder and devout liberal Ted Turner was offended on Ash Wednesday 2001 when he spotted some of his employees with ash marks on their foreheads. "What are you, a bunch of Jesus freaks?" Turner demanded. "You ought to be working for Fox." Not exactly calculated to inspire confidence in your job security. But Mr. Turner is so offended by Christians, he once suggested it would be good if the pope stepped on a land mine. Oh, and opponents of abortion are "bozos." "Christianity is a religion for losers," he explains.[14]

CBS's Bryant Gumbel was offended when the Family Research Council's Robert Knight had the audacity to come on the *Early Show* in 2000 to defend the U.S. Supreme Court's ruling upholding the Boy Scouts' First Amendment right to freely associate and ban homosexual scoutmasters. Gumbel was so offended that when he thought he was off camera, he could be clearly seen rising, removing his microphone, and exclaiming, "What a f---ing idiot!" Brent Bozell, president and founder of the Media Research Center, suggested that CBS could stand for Christian Bashing System.[15] In his book *Bias*, Bernard Goldberg reports that CBS producer Roxanne Russell called Christian activist and presidential candidate Gary Bauer "the little nut from the Christian group."[16]

Bozell notes that the Catholic Church seems to top the list of offensiveness, especially to the media:

The Roman Catholic Church is viewed as an unhip anachronism—it has the poor taste to have rules and insist its members follow them—and has emerged as a major target for the media's religious bigots. . . . There is nothing, it seems, to which the media won't give credence when attacks on the Catholic Church are concerned.[17]

Examples abound: *Newsweek*'s Eleanor Clift's likening conservative U.S. bishops to the Taliban; the media's "feeding frenzy" on the issue of sexual abuse committed by priests; the *New York Times*' Maureen Dowd's calling American priests "a perp walk of sacramental perverts"; and on and on.

According to *U.S. News & World Report*'s columnist John Leo:

In painting and sculpture, the bashing of Christian symbols is so mainstream that it's barely noticed. . . .

Recent examples include the Virgin Mary encased in a condom, Mary in pink panties with breasts partially exposed, an Annunciation scene with the Archangel Gabriel giving Mary a coat hanger for an abortion, Mary pierced with a phallic pipe, and many satirical version[s] of the Last Supper (one in the Brooklyn Museum show features a bare-breasted female Jesus). . . .

The obliviousness of elite opinion on this issue is astonishing. A *New York Times* editorial on the

Brooklyn controversy informed us that "cultural experimentation and transgression are not threats to civility but part of the texture and meaning of daily life." Transgression aimed at Christian believers may be a walk in the park to the *Times*, but the paper clearly doesn't feel that way when the transgression is aimed at groups it cares more about. . . . This is known as a double standard.[18]

And it's the *church* that's offensive? Leo's examples remind us again of Schaeffer's steps: Philosophy → Art → Music → General Culture → Theology. Following are a few more examples of "offensive" Christianity.

Corpus Christi

Don't go to this play thinking it's something devoutly religious. Here's the Catholic League's Bill Donohue's review:

If only the *New York Times* thought of Catholics as if we were all gay, we'd have no problem with the newspaper. The vile play, which they love—not for artistic purposes but for its assault on Catholicism—features the Jesus character, Joshua, saying to his apostles things like, "F--- your mother, F--- your father, F--- God." The Jesus-character is dubbed "King of the Queers" and the script is replete with sexual and scatological comments. At one point, a character named Philip asks the Jesus-figure to perform fellatio on him.[19]

The *Times* dismissed protests of the play as "homophobia."

Merry F---ing Christmas

Don't complain to Comedy Central about vile programming. The Catholic League complained about this Christmas show, "and we were rewarded with 'Sacrilegious Sunday' in 2006 in which anti-Christian programs aired all day on Christmas Eve," complete with a hooker, lesbian nuns, and Denis Leary:

> I was raised Catholic. We believe Mary was a virgin and Jesus ended up walking on water, creating a bottomless jug of wine and rising from the dead. Oh, yeah, and Tom Cruise is crazy. Listen, Christmas is built on a line of bulls---. Do I believe there was a baby Jesus? You bet your a-- I do. But I believe that nine months before he was born someone sure as s--- b---ed the hell out of his mom.[20]

The Catholic League should relax. According to the rationale of the *Times*, this is all just "a part of the texture and meaning of daily life."

Christian Derangement Syndrome

After reading this rant by columnist Bob Norman, you can almost understand how George W. Bush must have felt when he heard any of Cindy Sheehan's or Code Pink's over-the-top tirades against him, or when he read the reaction from the dailies when he named Jesus as his favorite philosopher:

> Religious fanatics are threatening to take away our peace and our freedom. They hate our open society and want to send us back to the Stone Age, where we'd be forced to live strictly by the rules of an out-dated religious text. Even as I write this, they are planning to take us over, and if they get their way, they'll execute many of us for violating their archaic moral code. They'll rule those left behind with a bloody iron fist. I am, of course, talking about the Christian extremists. The underbelly of the Christian Right is as scary as anything that ever dwelled in a Tora Bora cave. If September 11 taught us anything, it should have been to distrust religious fundamental-ists of any kind, to leave them stranded on the banks of the political mainstream where they belong.[21]

Christian Terrorists

Remember those 2001 anthrax attacks in the nation's capital? You probably didn't know those were the work of Christian conservatives—unless you listened to National Public Radio. On January 22, 2002, NPR's David Kestenbaum built a circumstantial case that the

Reverend Lou Sheldon's Traditional Values Coalition (TVC) might have had a motive for the anthrax letters received by Democrat senators Tom Daschle and Patrick Leahy. Seems just before the attacks the TVC had issued a press release criticizing Daschle and Leahy for trying to remove "so help me God" from the presidential oath. Kestenbaum implied the FBI might be looking into it. NPR eventually had to apologize for this inane report—one year later.[22]

You would think that mainstream media organs would look at their plummeting popularity and rapidly shrinking revenue and give serious thought to why a growing number of the Americans are turning elsewhere for their news. This would make sense if for no other reason than a pragmatic pursuit of the almighty dollar. But arrogance and elitism are not so easily overcome. The mainstream media believes that America must be delivered from Christianity for the good of us all. They're not about to let profits get in the way of their ideology.

6.

WHAT THE NUMBERS SAY

Like a mighty army moves the church of God; brothers, we are treading where the saints have trod. We are not divided, all one body we, one in hope and doctrine, one in charity.

—Lyrics from the 19th-century hymn,
"Onward, Christian Soldiers"

Is there a disconnect between average Americans and their government over the topic of religion in the public square? You could say that—and you'd be making an understatement. Take the Georgetown Cover-up, where White House staff requested religious symbols be shrouded before President Obama spoke at the Catholic university. According to a Zogby public opinion survey, only a little over a third (36 percent) of a particular group of citizens approved of that action.[1] Nearly two-thirds either disapproved (48 percent) or weren't sure about it (16 percent). Who are these people? Republicans? John McCain voters? No.

They are people who voted for Barack Obama in the 2008 presidential election. Disapproval was even stronger among other groups. "Moderates," for example, disapproved 3 to 1 (67 to 22 percent). Disapproval among conservatives was nearly unanimous (97 to 2 percent). Among all groups, 70 percent disapproved, only 20 percent approved, and 9 percent were not sure.

Although Barack Obama won the support of many people of faith, public opinion sampling has tended to show that Obama the person is considerably more popular than many of his specific policies. It also tends to show that religion in America is a mixed bag of various beliefs and wide-ranging levels of devotion to them. According to the Pew Forum on Religion & Public Life, America is "among the most religiously dynamic and diverse countries in the world."[2] The Pew Forum said in its "Religious Landscape Survey":

> From the beginning of the Colonial period, religion has been a major factor in shaping the identity and values of the American people. Despite predictions that the United States would follow Europe's path toward widespread secularization, the U.S. population remains highly religious in its beliefs and practices, and religion continues to play a prominent role in American public life.[3]

Snapshot of Faith

Some of the impetus for Pew's survey came from the fact that of all the demographic slicing and dicing done by the

U.S. Census Bureau on other characteristics, it is prohibited by law from asking about religious affiliation of the citizenry. So, the Pew organization interviewed 35,000 Americans in 2008 to try to fill this void. It found, for example, that more than one quarter of Americans (28 percent) have left the faith in which they were raised. The Landscape Survey also found that "the United States is on the verge of becoming a minority Protestant country" for the first time in its history, with barely 51 percent claiming affiliation with a Protestant denomination. That's down from more than 60 percent in the 1970s and 1980s. The greatest numerical growth has been in the ranks of the "unaffiliated."[4]

Other highlights:

- Men are significantly more likely than women to claim no religious affiliation. Nearly 20 percent of men say they have no formal religious affiliation, compared with roughly 13 percent of women.

- Among people who are married, nearly 37 percent are married to a spouse with a different religious affiliation. (This figure includes Protestants who are married to another Protestant from a different denominational family, such as a Baptist who is married to a Methodist.) Hindus and Mormons are the most likely to be married (78 percent and 71 percent, respectively) and to be married to someone of the same religion (90 percent and 83 percent, respectively).

- Mormons and Muslims are the groups with the largest families; more than 20 percent of Mormon adults and 15 percent of Muslim adults in the United States have three or more children living at home.
- The Midwest most closely resembles the religious makeup of the overall population. The South, by a wide margin, has the heaviest concentration of members of evangelical Protestant churches. The Northeast has the greatest concentration of Catholics, and the West has the largest proportion of unaffiliated people, including the largest proportion of atheists and agnostics.
- Of all the major racial and ethnic groups in the United States, black Americans are the most likely to report a formal religious affiliation. Even among those blacks who are unaffiliated, roughly 75 percent belong to the "religious unaffiliated" category (that is, they say that religion is either somewhat or very important in their lives), compared with slightly more than 33 percent of the unaffiliated population overall.
- Members of Baptist churches account for over 30 percent of all Protestants and close to 20 percent of the total U.S. adult population. Baptists also account for nearly 67 percent of members of historically black Protestant churches.[5]

To see where the trends are leading, look at the younger segment of the population, which is the dominant group in waiting. The numbers suggest an increasing secularization:

> Adults under age 30 are more than three times as likely as those aged 70 and older to be unaffiliated with any particular religion (25 vs. 8 percent). The younger group is also more likely than the adult population as a whole to be atheist or agnostic (7 vs. 4 percent).[6]

There is, however, one other factor—Islam. Religiously "unaffiliated" and Muslim correlate with youth much to the same degree. According to the Religious Landscape Survey, about three in ten unaffiliated and Muslim (31 and 29 percent, respectively) are under the age of thirty, and more than seven in ten (71 and 77 percent, respectively) are under age fifty.[7] What are we to make of this? The culture is apparently headed for even greater polarization over the church-state issue with ever-stronger opposing forces of secularism and religious fundamentalism pulling on the center. One group will be striving to prove Bill Maher right when he says the future does not belong to religion, while the other group works just as hard to prove him wrong. If not resolved, the big question is whether the center can hold.

Celebrate Diversity

To complicate things further, Pew researchers Brian Grim and David Masci warn it is not strictly accurate to equate all unaffiliated with nonreligious or secular. A large portion of even these folks, they say, call religion somewhat important or very important in their lives. And it's a big group—16 percent of the adult population—making them the fourth largest "religious" tradition in the United States.[8]

There are some other surprises and eye-openers in the Religious Landscape Survey, especially among the smaller minority religions of Judaism (2 percent), Buddhism (0.7 percent), Islam (0.6 percent), and Hinduism (0.4 percent). Three of the four groups—Jews, Hindus, and Buddhists—report much higher levels of postgraduate education than the general population, and Jews and Hindus also report much higher income levels. Muslims are the most racially diverse. More than one in three Muslims are white, roughly 25 percent black, 20 percent are Asian, and 20 percent are other races.[9]

The research also shows that America's central heartland, the Midwest, is nearly identical to the overall religious makeup of the entire population:

About a quarter (26 percent) of residents of the Midwest are members of an evangelical Protestant church, about one in five (22 percent) are members of a main-line Protestant church, nearly a quarter (24 percent) are Catholic, and 16 percent are unaffiliated.[10]

The remainder of the religious landscape looks like this:

The Northeast has more Catholics (37 percent) than other regions and has the fewest number of people affiliated with evangelical Protestant churches (13 percent). Northeasterners also are much more likely to be Jewish (4 percent are Jewish) than people living in other regions. By contrast, fully half of members of evangelical Protestant churches live in the South, compared with only 10 percent in the Northeast and 17 percent in the West. The vast majority of Mormons (76 percent) live in the West, with the highest concentration in the state of Utah. The West also has the largest proportion of people unaffiliated with any particular religion (21 percent), including the largest number of atheists and agnostics.[11]

Only 1.6 percent of the adult population is atheist. Mormons account for 1.7 percent. Various Orthodox churches account for 0.6 percent. Jehovah's Witnesses are 0.7 percent. Of those, more than two-thirds were converts from another faith or previously unaffiliated. Altogether, more than a quarter of American adults have left the faith in which they were raised in favor of another religion or no religion (not counting changes from one type of Protestantism to another).[12]

Gender and Family

The Religious Landscape Survey confirms what most churchgoers observe each Sunday: Women consistently outnumber men. Men are significantly more likely (20 percent) to claim no religious affiliation than women (13 percent), according to the Pew survey. Men are three times as likely (6 percent) to be atheist or agnostic than women (2 percent). Women outnumber men in both Protestantism and Catholicism by the same margin—54 to 46 percent— and nearly every denominational subgroup. In this, Christianity is exceptional. The reverse is the case with other major religions, including Judaism, Islam, Buddhism, and Hinduism.[13] The Pew Forum offers no explanation for this difference, but contrary to Rosie O'Donnell and friends, Christianity has far and away the best record for treatment of women and for women's rights.

Another way of looking into the future is to see who has the most children. Conversion growth may be highly desirable, but when it comes to religious groups, biological growth is the real engine.

Today large families are no longer the trademark of Catholics, but now Mormons and Muslims. Simple arithmetic dictates that families with two children are at "replacement rate" (i.e., no net gain or loss). Families with three or more children have positive net growth. Among all religious groups combined, 9 percent of U.S. households have three or more children, according to the Religious Landscape Survey. Catholics and Protestants are close to that norm at 11 percent and 8 percent, respectively. Mainline Protestant families are a bit below it at 6 percent, while evangelicals and black church families are on pace at 9 and 10 percent, respectively. Jewish families are close behind at 8 percent with three or more children.[14]

Way ahead of the race are Muslims at 15 percent and Mormons at 21 percent having three or more children. But these percentages apply to very small overall numbers, as Muslims comprise only 0.6 percent of the U.S. population and Mormons 1.7 percent. Other small groups, Buddhists and Hindus, are losing ground with only 4 percent and 3 percent having three or more children, respectively.

The bad news here for Christians is that what should be a stable situation in terms of biological growth actually translates into net losses when the attrition rate of 25 percent is factored in. This is the rate of conversion to another faith, no faith, or unaffiliated—something that's rare for Mormons and almost unheard-of for Muslims.

Take the unfortunate case of Rifqa Bary, a seventeen-year-old high school cheerleader from Columbus, Ohio, who fled to Florida in July 2009 out of fear she would be harmed or killed by her Sri Lankan Muslim family because of her conversion to Christianity. "If I had stayed in Ohio, I wouldn't be alive," she told reporters. "In 150 generations in [my] family, no one has known Jesus. I am the first—imagine the honor in killing me."[15] Muslim girls who bring shame to their families are in danger of losing their lives through "honor killing." That is why conversion among Muslims is almost nonexistent.

Some Good News

When the Gallup organization began surveying public opinion in 1948, it pegged the percentage of Christians in America at 91 percent. It stayed at that level until the 1960s, when a slow, steady decline began, continuing to the present, where it stands at 77 percent. Most of that loss apparently occurred among Protestants and other non-Catholic Christians, who have declined from 70 to 55 percent. Meanwhile, the Catholic population has remained relatively stable in the 20s, peaking in the 1970s at 30 percent and declining to 22 percent by 2008, where it had been prior to the 1970s.[16] There is little doubt that waves of largely Catholic Mexican immigrants have contributed to this stability.

Like Pew, Gallup has documented significant growth in the percentage of Americans reporting "no religion." In 1948, only 2 percent stated "no religion." That number began growing in the 1970s and now stands at 12 percent. (Pew's "unaffiliated" is a bit broader term than Gallup's "no religion.") Meanwhile, over the same period, the "other" category (Muslim, Buddhist, Hindu, etc.) has climbed from near 0 to 7 percent.[17] Gallup reports there are many possible reasons for this tremendous growth in the nonreligious:

> The United States remains a dominantly Christian nation. More than three-quarters of all Americans identify as Christian. And the majority of those who identify with any religion say they are Christian in some form or another. . . . The big shift has apparently been the out-migration of those whose parents may have identified with a specific Christian religion, but who upon growing up have become more likely to tell a survey interviewer that they have no specific religious identity. . . . It is possible that Americans who previously would have identified themselves with the religion of their upbringing now feel free to tell a survey interviewer that they have no religious identity.[18]

Such choice is a fundamental right in American democracy, but again not one easily enjoyed by Rifqa Bary and thousands of others like her.

Gallup also noted that religious identification by itself says little about the relevance of that faith to the individual or how actively the individual practices it. One basic measure is actual weekly church attendance. By that measure, Catholics have become much more like Protestants in recent years, dropping from 75 to 45 percent over the past six decades. Weekly Protestant church attendance has been hovering in the low to mid-40s pretty much the entire time. Much of the Catholic drop occurred in the 1960s and 1970s, starting with younger Catholics and eventually spreading to all age groups before leveling off. Gallup found reasons for encouragement in some of this, especially the fact that Catholic attendance remains virtually unchanged since 1995:

> That's an extremely important finding given the upheaval in the U.S. Roman Catholic Church caused by the sexual abuse scandals that erupted earlier this decade. Gallup polling in 2002 and 2003 found a decline in the percentage of Catholics saying they had attended church in the past week; however, attendance rebounded by the end of 2003 and has since remained on par with its pre-scandal level of 45 percent. . . . The good news for the Catholic Church is that the drop in attendance seems to have slowed or abated altogether in the last decade, spanning a most difficult period for the church around 2002, when attendance did suffer temporarily.
>
> U.S. Protestant church attendance has also been steady over the past decade, but is actually higher now than it was in the 1970s and 1980s, in part the result of a resurgence of regular attendance among young adults.[19]

Zogby Research

In 2010, Zogby International conducted a poll of more than 10,000 likely voters and found that 24 percent of them consider the endorsement of the Christian Coalition important on Election Day. Apply this percentage to the overall number of voters in America, and this comes to a sizeable 31 million voters. What's more, the poll found that 88 percent of these Christian Coalition voters think that the federal government has become so large and powerful that it poses an immediate threat to their rights and freedoms—clearly, Christians understand the inverse correlation between the size of government and individual freedom. When asked, 84 percent of these voters also preferred someone new be elected president over Barack Obama.

Public opinion polling also reveals differences among major faiths on important issues. Zogby asked various groups in April 2009 how they would regard a U.S. Supreme Court nominee who advocated taking international law into the decision-making process, including Islamic Sharia law and laws in socialist countries. Only 26 percent of Americans agree with such an approach, while 60 percent disagree (13 percent are not sure), according to Zogby. The results, broken out according to major faiths, other or unaffiliated, born-again, non-born-again Christians, and by frequency of church attendance:[20]

	Catholic	Protestant	Jewish	Other/None	Born-Again	xBorn-Again
Agree	24.5	22.1	49.6	37.3	14.0	27.9
Disagree	64.1	66.4	32.7	40.9	76.9	58.4
Not sure	11.4	11.6	17.7	21.9	9.2	13.6
Attend Services	Weekly+	Weekly	1–2/mo.	Holidays	Rarely	Never
Agree	22.7	16.3	21.7	28.2	30.7	40.5
Disagree	70.1	69.2	68.1	65.2	51.8	42.7
Not sure	7.2	14.5	10.2	6.6	17.5	16.9

Note the strong correlation of Christian identification—and frequent church attendance—with strong disagreement with U.S. judges relying on international law. More than three quarters (77 percent) of "Born-Again" believers reject this approach. The highest rate of un—decided (22 percent) is among "Other" and "None," which could be reflective of a general inability to make decisive judgments or commitments. The only group with a plurality agreeing with international law influencing Supreme Court justices is the Jewish community, a group with traditionally strong strains of political liberalism.

Another Zogby question from 2009: "While visiting Turkey recently, President Obama said America is not a Christian nation. Do you agree or disagree that the U.S. is a Christian nation?" The results:[21]

	Catholic	Protestant	Jewish	Other/None	Born-Again	xBorn-Again
Agree	46.0	40.5	25.0	34.1	36.5	44.8
Disagree	50.3	52.4	60.0	56.0	55.4	49.2
Not sure	3.7	7.1	15.0	9.9	8.1	6.0

Attend Services	Weekly+	Weekly	1–2/mo.	Holidays	Rarely	Never
Agree	36.5	39.8	49.9	45.3	41.7	38.2
Disagree	58.3	52.2	51.1	49.2	51.7	53.9
Not sure	5.2	8.0	7.0	5.5	6.6	7.9

By comparison, the totals for all Americans on this question were 41 percent agree, 52 percent disagree, and 7 percent not sure. It's hard to tell whether people take the question more as proscriptive—the way it should be—or descriptive, the way things are. Note that the Protestant response closely mirrors the national average for its responses. No big surprise there, as Protestants comprise a majority of the population. But Born-Again believers disagree more with the notion of America as a Christian nation. That should quickly put the lie to Rosie O'Donnell and others trying to sell the idea that evangelicals are all about setting up a "theocracy."

Another Zogby question: "In God We Trust is displayed over the Speaker's podium in the U.S. Capitol Building. In the new model of renovations, they have taken out In God We Trust. Should the In God We Trust inscription be kept or taken out?" The results:[22]

	Catholic	Protestant	Jewish	Other/None	Born-Again	xBorn-Again
Agree	78.9	81.7	37.4	39.7	91.8	72.7
Disagree	10.8	10.3	41.6	47.5	3.4	16.6
Not sure	10.3	8.1	20.9	12.8	4.8	10.7

Attend Services	Weekly+	Weekly	1–2/mo.	Holidays	Rarely	Never
Agree	89.3	87.2	76.8	73.5	67.4	37.3
Disagree	4.5	6.5	12.7	17.3	19.6	52.7
Not sure	6.2	6.3	10.5	9.3	13.0	10.0

"Prior to his appearance, presidential staff requested that the symbol of Jesus be covered up. Do you approve or disapprove of the White House's actions?" Results below.[23]

By comparison, among all Americans only 21 percent approved, 71 percent disapproved, and 9 percent are not

	Catholic	Protestant	Jewish	Other/None	Born-Again	xBorn-Again
Agree	12.0	16.6	54.0	38.6	6.3	25.1
Disagree	78.0	76.3	37.2	47.3	90.5	64.9
Not sure	10.0	7.0	8.8	14.0	3.2	10.0

Attend Services	Weekly+	Weekly	1–2/mo.	Holidays	Rarely	Never
Agree	11.6	7.9	18.5	17.8	25.6	41.9
Disagree	84.1	87.9	72.2	68.6	63.1	43.1
Not sure	4.3	4.3	9.3	13.7	11.3	15.0

sure. Again, Catholic, Born-Again, and frequent attenders disapproved most strongly.

To test the correlation between politics and religion, Zogby asked, "Which of the following party affiliations do you most identify with?" The results:[24]

	Catholic	Protestant	Jewish	Other/None	Born-Again	xBorn-Again
Dem.	36.7	37.2	38.3	43.1	33.8	41.3
Rep.	27.6	39.6	33.7	22.0	42.6	36.3
Lib.	1.4	3.3	5.4	8.8	2.5	4.3
Green	2.8	0.3	1.5	2.1	0.4	0.1
Const.	0.4	0.7	0	2.7	1.4	0
Ind.	12.3	9.9	18.1	6.4	9.3	10.2
Other	7.3	5.0	5.5	6.1	6.6	3.1
None	11.5	4.0	8.2	8.8	3.4	4.7

Attend Services	Weekly+	Weekly	1–2/mo.	Holidays	Rarely	Never
Dem.	42.3	35.8	35.0	39.2	43.0	37.2
Rep.	46.5	35.5	27.2	23.8	27.8	35.9
Lib.	1.5	1.5	5.1	23.0	2.1	3.6
Green	2.8	0.7	0.9	3.0	1.1	2.0
Const.	0.3	1.3	0	0	0	5.3
Ind.	3.0	7.2	18.1	7.5	12.4	7.1
Other	1.5	8.7	5.5	0.4	5.9	3.4
None	2.1	9.3	8.2	3.2	7.9	5.6

By comparison, among all Americans, 38 percent are Democrat, 33 percent are Republican, 4 percent are Libertarian, 1 percent are Green, 1 percent are Constitution Party, 10 percent are Independent, 6 percent are other, and 7 percent are none. What might be most remarkable here is the weakness of the religious correlation, especially in light of conventional wisdom. Protestant and Born-Again, for example, are the only groups with a Republican majority, but by smaller margins than might be expected. Jews are also closely split between Republican and Democrat, suggesting a fair number of liberal Republicans in the group.

Rasmussen Research

Rasmussen Reports has also delved into public opinion on some of these religion-political issues. It found many Americans took exception, for example, to presidential candidate Barack Obama's remarks about people in small towns who "cling to guns or religion or antipathy to people who aren't like them or anti-immigrant sentiment as a way to explain their frustrations." More than twice as many Americans (56 percent) disagreed with the future president as agreed (25 percent). Disagreement rose to 75 percent among conservatives. Strongest agreement, though still not a majority, came from liberals at 46 percent. Moderates disagreed 51 percent to 27 percent. Other slices of the data showed predictable trends—e.g., younger individuals, Democrats, and blacks tended to agree some-what more with the small-town slam, while older people and Republicans considered the remarks "elitist" and inappropriate.[25]

Rasmussen found strong support for continuing the practice of an inaugural prayer when Obama made the surprising choice of leading evangelical pastor Rick War-ren to pray at his January 2009 inauguration. Some gays expressed outrage, and atheist Michael Newdow sued, but overall the choice was considered a smart outreach to the other side. More than three-fourths (77 percent) of voters approved of continuing with the inaugural prayer tradition, while only 14 percent disapproved. Nine out of ten GOP voters (89 percent) and more than two-thirds of Democrats (71 percent) and unaffiliated (72 percent) approved. The choice of Warren himself produced inter-esting results. Far less than half of white voters (39 per-cent) approved of the choice, versus a majority of blacks (52 percent).[26]

Nearly 66 percent believe Christmas is still one of the nation's most important holidays, according to Rasmus-sen. That number rises for Republicans (77 percent) and African-Americans (70 percent) and drops for Democrats (56 percent) and whites (64 percent). One of the stranger disparities in responses is for men over the age of 40—72 percent approval—versus less than half of men under 40 (48 percent). Rasmussen also reported that most shop-pers still prefer to be greeted with "Merry Christmas" over "Happy Holidays."[27]

Sentiment for Easter is only about half as strong. Only 37 percent of adults consider Easter to be one of the nation's most important holidays—the top three being Christmas, Fourth of July, and Thanksgiving. The Easter numbers, naturally, rise for evangelicals, as 63 percent rank it at the top.

Yet, Rasmussen found that the "basics of Christianity" continue to enjoy strong support in America, as 80 percent of Americans believe in a historic Jesus who lived and walked the earth, and only 8 percent do not. A strong majority of Americans also believe that Jesus rose from the dead (75 percent) and that He was the Son of God who came to die for our sins (76 percent).[28]

Assorted other Rasmussen findings on faith in America:

- Forty-four percent of America's adults attend Christian church services at least twice a month, and 92 percent of these regular churchgoers believe the God of the Bible is the one true God.
- Eighteen percent of regular churchgoers read the Bible daily, 32 percent read Scripture several times a week, and 20 percent about once a week. However, 26 percent say they rarely or never read the Bible.
- Thirty-seven percent reflect on the meaning of Scripture in their lives on a daily basis.
- Forty-nine percent pray to seek guidance on a daily basis, and 43 percent pray to confess sins daily. Just 7 percent say they don't pray for guidance at all in

a typical week, and 13 percent don't pray to confess sins.

- Fifty percent of regular churchgoers attend a regular Bible study or participate in some other small-group activity within the church. Sixty-five percent volunteer for some form of service activities.

- Sixty-two percent of regular churchgoers consider themselves to be Born-Again Christians. This figure includes 91 percent of Evangelical Christians, 63 percent of other Protestants, and 25 percent of Catholics.

- Politically, 41 percent of regular churchgoers are Republicans, 34 percent are Democrats, and 25 percent are unaffiliated with either major party. Fifty-six percent are politically conservative, 23 percent moderate and 20 percent politically liberal.

What to Do?

Want to put an end to continual challenges to Christmas and other religious holiday displays, to students not being allowed to utter the name "Jesus" in a commencement address or to pray, to bans on any and all expressions of faith in public? If so, you're in good company with a majority of Americans. Peter Ferrara, chief counsel for the American Civil Rights Union, notes evidence from six major polling firms for a strong consensus—75 percent and above—for many of the issues we've been examining, including support for:

- "under God" in the Pledge of Allegiance
- Christmas trees and Menorahs on public property
- voluntary moments of silence in the public schools
- Ten Commandments posted in courthouses and other government buildings

And by similar margins they disapprove of:

- forced removal of crosses and other religious symbols from public property
- efforts to make sure no religious expression is permitted in a public building
- candidates and public officials who advocate removing all religious references and symbols from public buildings, land, or documents[29]

"What emerges from this pattern is that the ACLU secularist vision of the separation of church and state has support among the American people in the single digits," said Ferrara. "The American people consistently oppose this view by 10 to 1." Thus, Ferrara has proposed a powerfully simple Freedom of Religious Expression Amendment, stating: "Religious expression, freely chosen, in any public forum, venue or context, shall not constitute an establishment of religion under the First Amendment." He claims the case is compelling because legally "mere religious expression is nowhere near an establishment of religion."[30]

Despite overwhelming popularity, the bill has never made it out of Congress. A two-thirds vote in the House and Senate would be required to pass the constitutional amendment; then three-fourths of the fifty states would need to ratify it. Some claim that such an amendment would be overkill because, rightly interpreted, the First Amendment already guarantees these freedoms. Others say that's the very problem—the judiciary in too many cases has indicated an unwillingness to rightly interpret the First Amendment as originally intended, and the only way to fix that is constitutionally.

Whatever the case, it is clear that there may be no end in sight to the confusion short of some solution of this magnitude—or a national revival.

7.

THE WAR ON HOMESCHOOLING

The National Education Association believes that home schooling programs cannot provide the student with a comprehensive education experience. The Association believes that if parental preference home schooling study occurs, students enrolled must meet all state requirements. Instruction should be by persons who are licensed by the appropriate state education licensure agency, and a curriculum approved by the state department of education should be used. The Association further believes that such home schooling programs should be limited to the children of the immediate family, with all expenses being borne by the parents.

—*A Resolution adopted by National Education Association*

BY THE TURN of the century, approximately two million children were being homeschooled. To put that in perspective, this is more than the *combined* number of public school students in the following states in 2000: Alaska, Delaware, Hawaii, Idaho, Maine, Montana, Nebraska, North Dakota, Rhode Island, South Dakota, Vermont, and Wyoming. Comparing further, the national homeschool population was about the same as the public school population of Illinois—the fifth most populous state.

This is all very bad news for our nation's public education establishment, which not only resents the superior academic results of homeschoolers, but also their tremendous numerical growth. In addition, they are particularly chafed by the fact that a significant number of homeschoolers are serious Christians. The best estimates are that conservative evangelical and fundamentalist Christians, together with faithful, practicing Catholics, comprise about two-thirds of the families in America who have chosen to homeschool their children.

The leftist elites have begun the drumbeat to reverse all of these trends. Of course, their central argument is that government intervention into homeschooling is necessary for the "protection" of children. But what exactly do homeschooled children need protection from?

Robin West, a professor at Georgetown University School of Law, describes the dangers she sees for homeschooled children in a thinly disguised anti-Christian screed published by the *Philosophy and Public Policy Quarterly*:

> Child-raising that is relentlessly authoritarian risks instilling what developmental psychologists call "ethical servility": a failure to mature morally beyond the recognition of the duties of obedience. In the most devoutly fundamentalist households, ethical servility

might not be regarded as a bad outcome; it may be a desired goal. But whether a virtue or a disability, homeschooling—where the parents have full responsibility for the extent and substance of the child's education as well as upbringing—clearly multiplies the risk.[1]

In other words, if children are brought up to believe in certain absolute truths, they are ethically servile. Only those who "advance" to the level of moral relativism—rejecting the idea that there are such things as absolute truth and absolute values—avoid the danger of "ethical servility."

Any pretense that West is making an informed and reasoned argument disappears when she continues her rant against Christian home educators.

The average homeschooling family may have a higher income than the average non-homeschooler, as was recently reported by *USA Today*. The radically fundamentalist "movement" family, however, is considerably poorer than the population, and it is the participants in these movements . . . that are the hardcore of the homeschooling movement. The husbands and wives in these families feel themselves under a religious compulsion to have large families, a homebound and submissive wife and mother who are responsible for the schooling of the children, and only one breadwinner. These families are not living in romantic, rural, self-sufficient farmhouses; they are in trailer parks, 1,000 square-foot homes, houses owned by relatives, and some on tarps in fields or parking lots. Their lack of job skills, passed from one generation to the next, depresses the community's overall economic health and their state's tax base.

Her wild assertions lack a single reference to any source of evidence for these spurious, bigoted claims. The furor that would arise if she described a poor, ethnic minority in this fashion would terminate her career at any respectable educational institute. But unfounded and irrational criticism of conservative Christians is not a disqualifier, but a badge of honor in elitist educational circles.

Another elitist critic of the homeschooling movement is found on the faculty at Stanford University—Robert Reich, a political theorist. Although he writes more elegantly and with considerably more diplomacy than Professor West, Reich shares her alarm over the fact that homeschooled children may fail to be taught the doctrines of multiculturalism. The central concept of multiculturalism is the assertion that there are many versions of truth and no one system of thinking is the "Truth." Reich believes that it is a duty of the government to ensure that all children are taught to embrace multiculturalism.

"Children deserve as a matter of justice an education that cultivates their autonomy and that is multicultural," Reich argues.[2]

Reich recommends a variety of legal constraints on

homeschooling to ensure that all children receive his idealized form of multicultural education:

> [B]ecause the state must ensure that the school environment provides exposure to and engagement with values and beliefs other than those of a child's parents, the state should require parents to use multicultural curricula that provide such exposure and engagement. They must, in other words, convince relevant public officials that the educational environment of the home fits somewhere with the ambit of liberal multicultural education.[3]

Reich and West, as typical representatives of the establishment elites, openly admit that they believe the government has a duty to ensure that children embrace the philosophy of multicultural liberalism—and the moral relativism upon which it is built. Neither of them seems to be the least bit bothered by their rejection of one of the greatest statements regarding intellectual freedom ever written by the Supreme Court:

> If there is any fixed star in our constitutional constellation, it is that no official, high or petty, can prescribe what shall be orthodox in politics, nationalism, religion, or other matters of opinion or force citizens to confess by word or act their faith therein. If there are any circumstances which permit an exception, they do not now occur to us.[4]

American homeschoolers are not alone in arousing the antagonism of the educational elites. In 2009, the English government released a comprehensive report on home education written by a man named Graham Badman. After reading his report, homeschoolers found his name to be fitting.

He contended that homeschooling needed to be subject to stringent regulations, including government interrogations of children on a wide variety of subjects including an assessment of the child's wishes regarding his or her education.

Badman also urged new substantive requirements be adopted to define what is "suitable" for the content of a child's education. He cited Article 29 of the United Nations Convention on the Rights of the Child as the standard for guiding such new requirements.

This article requires children to be taught:

- the development of respect for human rights and fundamental freedoms, and for the principles enshrined in the Charter of the United Nations;
- the development of respect for the child's parents, his or her own cultural identity, language and values, for the national values of the country in which the child is living, the country from which he or she may originate, and for civilizations different from his or her own;
- the preparation of the child for responsible life in a free society, in the spirit of understanding, peace,

tolerance, equality of sexes, and friendship among all peoples, ethnic, national and religious groups and persons of indigenous origin; The development of respect for the natural environment.

While most Americans would embrace many of the ideas in this list, few would willingly embrace the idea that they were responsible to teach children a list of values dictated by the UN. This is especially true when the UN—and their fellow multicultural liberals like West and Reich—would be in charge of defining the meaning of the terms and determining whether any particular program measured up to the UN standards.

In a 2006 treatise entitled *The U.N. Convention on the Rights of the Child: An Analysis of Treaty Provisions and Implications of U.S. Ratification,*[5] advocates of this treaty make this clear and bold declaration concerning the meaning of these sections: "Article 29(1)(b) through (e) directs state parties to instill *particular* values in children through education" (emphasis added).

The UN Committee on the Rights of the Child says that this section "requires the fundamental reworking of curricula to include the various aims of education and the systematic revision of textbooks." Retaining a nation's current values would be inappropriate. The UN says: "Approaches which do no more than seek to superimpose the aims and values of the article on the existing system without encouraging any deeper changes are clearly inadequate."

The American Bar Association (ABA), which *endorses* the UNCRC, has revealed the clearly anti-Christian meaning of all of these UN requirements. The ABA says that Christian schools, which reject alternate worldviews and teach that Christianity is the only true religion, "fly in the face" of Article 29.[6] It is also clear that the UN standards prohibit all parents—homeschooling or otherwise—and all churches from teaching children an intolerant form of religion.

If the internationalist elite were to have its way, churches, schools, and parents would be permitted to teach that Jesus is one way to God. They could even teach that Jesus is the best way to God for our family or our church. What they could *not* teach is that Jesus is the only way to God for all of mankind.

Homeschooling in the Courtroom

The homeschooling movement is one of the most remarkable examples of the progress of freedom in recent American history. The statist crowd that urges us all to believe that *"it takes a village to raise a child"* likes to pretend that children will not be raised properly without an army of government-paid nannies intervening in the lives of children on a regular basis.

According to Michael Farris, one of the pioneers of the modern homeschooling movement and the founder of the Home School Legal Defense Association, "In the early

1980s, professional educators simply asserted that it would be impossible for parents to successfully deliver proper academic content to their own children. After all, only trained professionals with state credentials were capable of teaching children."

In the nearly three decades that have followed, the academic success of homeschooling has become common public knowledge. Homeschoolers are always disproportionately represented at the top of the National Spelling Bee, the Geography Bee, and other national academic contests. Homeschoolers are winning admission to the most elite colleges in the county. And full-blown academic studies of homeschooling students on standardized achievement tests routinely reveal stunningly high results. The *average* homeschooled child scores as well on these tests as the students who are at the *honor society* level in the public schools.

Farris tells a revealing story from the early days of homeschooling.

I represented a family in Pennsylvania whose daughter was in the latter stages of elementary school. She had spent a couple years in the public school and was considered to be on the edge of being "learning disabled." The parents sought permission from the school system to begin homeschooling their daughter.

After two years of successful home education, the girl's test scores were very high. In fact, the school district wrote the parents saying that the daughter was now "gifted and talented." And when they applied to continue homeschooling for the third year, the school district denied their request because the parents, the school officials said, were incapable of teaching a gifted and talented child.

To make good on their threat they filed criminal charges against the parents to force the girl back into the public school system.

Farris drafted a federal civil rights lawsuit against the school district and sent the draft to the school officials. All charges were dropped.

Many other families faced similar threats of criminal prosecution for daring to stand upon their constitutional rights as parents to direct the upbringing and education of their children. And the government arguments against homeschooling would, at times, border on the ridiculous.

A case that went to the Supreme Court of North Dakota against the Raymond Larsen family illustrates the inane nature of many government arguments. At the time, North Dakota required all children to be taught by state-certified teachers—including those being taught at home by their parents. Neither of the Larsen parents were certified teachers, so school officials filed truancy because the Larsens continued homeschooling despite their threats.

HSLDA and Farris filed a constitutional defense to the charges, arguing that the government's interest in education was limited to the issues of literacy and self-sufficiency. Achievement testing conclusively demonstrated that the Larsen children were far ahead of their public school peers on the criteria that public education officials use to measure progress toward these goals.

But the lawyers for the government were not satisfied. Farris describes their arguments:

> The prosecutor's brief in the Supreme Court of North Dakota contended that the requirement of a state certified teacher furthered two additional goals. First, he claimed that children needed to learn lessons beyond the classroom, including lessons to be taught by bullies on the playground. Second, he claimed that if children did not attend a public school classroom with a certified teacher, they might miss out on the opportunity to have eye examinations.

"As to the first argument," Farris continued, "I simply answered that one could only hope that the government was not contending that the certified teachers were the actual bullies on the playground. But unless there was a real connection between the bullies and certification, the argument was irrelevant.

"The second argument was even more hilarious in the context of our case," said Farris. "The government was arguing that children needed to come to public schools to get eye exams in a case where Mrs. Larsen was a registered nurse and Dr. Raymond Larsen, M.D. was one of the few eye surgeons in all of North Dakota."

While the Supreme Court of North Dakota gave no credence to the arguments of the prosecutor, they simply refused to recognize the constitutional rights of home-schooling parents and ruled against the Larsens and many other parents in that state.

Ultimately, the national homeschooling movement held a rally on the steps of the North Dakota state capitol building called the "Bismarck Tea Party." Thousands of tea bags were handed to state legislators, government officials, the governor, and whoever else wandered by that day. On every bag were the words "The Consent of the Governed for Homeschoolers, Too." The protest worked, and the North Dakota legislature enacted far more lenient legislation not long afterwards.

Another landmark homeschooling case was decided by the Supreme Court of Michigan in 1993. Although in the early 1980s numerous states had required all teaching to be done by state-certified teachers, only Michigan, Iowa, and North Dakota clung to that statist standard into the 1990s.

Mark and Chris DeJonge were charged with the crime of truancy for refusing to send their children to an institutional school in violation of this teacher's certification statute. Like many before them, the DeJonges raised a constitutional defense based on religious freedom and parental rights.

They contended that the right of parents to choose an educational path for their children was a fundamental right and that the burden was on the government to prove that children would not learn unless taught by certified teachers. Farris, who represented the DeJonges before the Michigan Supreme Court, pointed out that the government submitted no evidence demonstrating that teacher's certification was necessary for educational success while the DeJonge family had proven that their children were well above grade level on standardized tests even though they were taught by Mrs. DeJonge, who lacked a state teaching license.

By a 4 to 3 vote, the Michigan high court ruled that the law requiring certified teachers was unconstitutional in the face of a claim for religious freedom and parental rights.

As the legal barriers to homeschooling continued to drop in the face of the legal and political efforts of homeschooling organizations like HSLDA and the numerous and effective state home education associations, more and more families began to homeschool their children.

In California, there were approximately 200,000 children being homeschooled in 2008. The rights of all of these children and all of their parents were imperiled by a "secretive" legal proceeding that led to an astonishing decision by the First Circuit of the California Court of Appeal in February of that year.

Another family was charged with a form of child neglect arising from an incident when one of their children ran away from home. They were longtime homeschoolers. They were not members of Home School Legal Defense Association and were therefore represented in juvenile court by court-appointed lawyers who were very experienced in that field but had no experience in defending homeschooling cases. Since all juvenile proceedings of this nature are confidential, no one in the leadership of the homeschooling movement had any idea that this case was in the court system.

Even though homeschooling was not a central feature in the initial matter, the social workers began to complain to the court about the family's home education. The trial judge said that the family had a right to homeschool and he was not going to rule otherwise. He used the term "absolute right"—although, a fair reading of the transcript would indicate that he meant to say "fundamental right," which is a more appropriate and defensible ruling.

The government appealed his decision to the Court of Appeal in Los Angeles. The judges were incensed at his use of the term "absolute right." They held that not only was there no absolute right, but that the statutes of California banned homeschooling and there was no constitutional right to homeschool at all.

Most important, the Court did not limit their decision to this one family; all homeschooling in California by everyone was declared to be illegal unless the parents possessed a state teaching credential. This decision was released to the public—the first notice that anyone had that this case was in the works.

Gary Kreep, of the United States Justice Foundation, agreed to represent the family in court. In the meantime, Michael Farris and Jim Mason from HSLDA prepared a motion for rehearing that Gary submitted to the Court of

Appeal. The brief argued that the Court had improperly relied on a fifty-year-old decision in reaching the conclusion that homeschooling was illegal in California. Farris and Mason described in depth all of the statutory and legal changes that had taken place in the intervening half century.

To everyone's amazement, the Court granted a new hearing and an avalanche of legal assistance descended upon the Court. The academic, social, and legal progress of the homeschooling movement was clearly portrayed to the Court in a nearly unprecedented team effort from a great number of conservative litigating organizations. Even governor Arnold Schwarzenegger and attorney general of California Jerry Brown filed briefs supporting the legitimacy of home education.

In June 2008, the Court totally reversed itself, saying that homeschooling was legal in California and recognizing that parents indeed have constitutional rights to direct their children's education. While the family was sent back for further hearings about the suitability of their actual educational program, the rest of California could breathe easy because their rights had been vindicated.

Many families were afraid that their children would be forced back into the public schools of California, replete with all of the educational and moral failures that are so evident in that system. Thousands of families seriously considered leaving California if the decision was not reversed. Thankfully, freedom prevailed and homeschooling continues to flourish in the Golden State.

Homeschoolers—along with Christian schools and all faithful families and churches—represent a clear and present danger to liberal multiculturalists who want all children to be indoctrinated in their worldview.

Children who are taught at home are not likely to think that the purpose of government is to supply them with their needs and desires. Instead, they readily embrace the concept that the purpose of government is to protect life, liberty, and property.

Socialism and multiculturalism needs children who have been dependent upon state services from an early age. The values and practices of homeschooling will remain a target for the people who want to coerce all of us to join their centralized, amoral utopia—for our own good, of course.

The fight to save our Christian heritage from not only being expunged from our current lives, but also white-washed from the history books, begins with teaching our children the truth. As we've seen throughout this book, so long as there are Americans alive who understand the true origins of our American society and culture, there will be Americans at the ready to fight back against those who would rewrite history.

★ ★ ★

If you want to join the fight to save Christianity in America, go to: www.AmericasWarOnChristianity.com

ENDNOTES

Chapter 1

[1] Deacon Keith Fournier, "We Hold These Truths: Our Dependence on God," *Catholic Online*, July 3, 2009, http://www.catholic.org/politics/story.php?id=33976.

[2] Edwin Mora, "House Committee Approves Engraving 'In God We Trust' in Capitol Visitor Center," *CNS News*, June 11, 2009, http://www.cnsnews.com/news/print/49444.

[3] "History of 'In God We Trust,'" U.S. Department of the Treasury, http://www.treas.gov/education/fact-sheets/currency/in-god-we-trust.shtml.

[4] Tom Gibb, "Minister Reprises 'Under God' Sermon," Pittsburgh *Post-Gazette*, August 19, 2002, http://www.post-gazette.com/nation/20020819pledge0819p1.asp.

[5] David L. Hudson Jr., "Pledge of Allegiance," Religious Liberty in Public Schools, http://www.firstamendmentcenter.org/rel_liberty/publicschools/topic.aspx?topic=pledge_of_allegiance2.

[6] Reverend George Docherty, "One Nation Under God," The New York Avenue Presbyterian Church, http://www.nyapc.org/congregation/Sermon_Archives/?month=1954-02.

[7] Lindsay Perna, "Atheists Sue to Stop 'In God We Trust' in Capitol Visitor's Center," *USA Today*, July 17, 2009.

[8] *Wikipedia*, s.v. "Roy Moore," http://en.wikipedia.org/wiki/Judge_Roy_Moore.

[9] "Ten Commandments Monument Moved," *CNN*, November 14, 2003, http://www.cnn.com/2003/LAW/08/27/ten.commandments/.

[10] "Kentucky Counties Fined $400,000 for Posting Ten Commandments," March 18, 2009, http://www.guardian.co.uk/world/2009/mar/18/kentucky-ten-commandments-fines.

[11] "Cross Displayed by Christian Group Deemed 'Blatantly Christian' and 'Offensive" at Chesapeake City Park,' Alliance Defense Fund, June 30, 2008, http://www.alliancedefensefund.org/news/story.aspx?cid=4588.

[12] "Crosses, Bibles Banned from Hospital Chapel," *WorldNetDaily*, April 8, 2009, http://www.worldnetdaily.com/index.php?fa=PAGE.view&pageId=94306.

[13] Bob, Unruh, "'Jesus' T-shirt Becomes Factor in 'Hate Crimes' Argument," *WorldNetDaily*, June 2, 2009, http://www.worldnetdaily.com/index.php?fa=PAGE.view&pageId=99927.

[14] "What's Wrong with Thought Crime (Hate Crime)Laws?" Family Research Council, http://www.frc.org/content/q--a-whats-wrong-with-thought-crime-hate-crime-laws--.

[15] J. Matt Barber, "Congress Should Repeal, Not Pass, Hate Crimes Laws," May 27, 2009, http://www.renewamerica.com/columns/mbarber/090527.

[16] Bob Unruh, "Praying 'in Jesus' Name' Elevated to Supremes," *WorldNetDaily*, October 23, 2008, http://www.wnd.com/index.php?fa=PAGE.view&pageId=78877.

[17] "State Bans 'Jesus' from Troopers' Prayers," *WorldNetDaily*, September 25, 2008, http://www.wnd.com/index.php?fa=PAGE .view&pageId=76196.

[18] "Navy Chaplain Being Booted from Service," *WorldNetDaily*, March 1, 2007, http://www.wnd.com/news/article .asp?ARTICLE_ID=54498.

[19] Ibid.

[20] Russell Goldman, "Iowa Town Renames Good Friday to 'Spring Holiday,'" *ABC News*, March 29, 2010.

[21] John Woolley and Gerhard Peters, *The American Presidency Project*, http://www.presidency.ucsb.edu/ws/index.php?pid=16515.

[22] "The Six Articles of the Code of Conduct," http://www .vetshome.com/military_code_of_conduct.htm.

[23] Ron Strom, "Wiccans Meeting on Air Force Base," *WorldNet-Daily*, January 26, 2005, http://www.wnd.com/index .php?pageId=28640.

[24] Stephen Adams, "The Architecture of a Smear," *Citizen* magazine, November 2005.

[25] Ibid.

[26] "Catholic Diocese Sues Conn. over Lobbying Laws," Associated Press, June 1, 2009, http://www.firstamendmentcenter.org/ news.aspx?id=21648.

[27] Drew Zahn, "Churches Outraged at State's Interference," *WorldNetDaily*, March 10, 2009, http://www.wnd.com/index .php?fa=PAGE.view&pageId=91352.

[28] The American Society for the Defense of Tradition, Family, and Property, "Leave the Church Alone!" March 10, 2009, http://www.tfp.org/tfp-home/catholic-perspective/ leave-the-church-alone.html.

[29] Drew Zahn, "State Moves to Restrict Catholics in Politics," *WorldNetDaily*, June 1, 2009, http://www.wnd.com/index.php?fa=PAGE.printable&pageId=99836.

[30] "Conn. Attorney General Criticizes 'Serious Constitutional Concerns' in Anti-Church Lobbying Inquiry," Catholic News Agency, July 7, 2009, http://www.catholicnewsagency.com/new.php?n=16476.

[31] Bob Unruh, "Court to Government: OK to Diss Catholics," *WorldNetDaily*, June 5, 2009, http://www.wnd.com/index.php?fa=PAGE.printable&pageId=100140.

[32] Drew Zahn, "Court Sentences Bishop for Ringing Church Bells," *WorldNetDaily*, June 5, 2009, http://www.wnd.com/index.php?pageId=100277.

[33] Ibid.

[34] "Police Repeatedly Raid Church to Stop 'Praise and Worship' Music," Thomas More Law Center, March 11, 2008, http://www.thomasmore.org/qry/page.taf?id=19&_function=detail&sbtblct_uid1=312.

[35] Chelsea Schilling, "Victory against Gospel Ban in Public Park," *WorldNetDaily*, May 8, 3009, http://www.wnd.com/index.php?fa=PAGE.view&pageId=97360.

[36] Bob Unruh, "San Diego Withdraws Bible Study Warning," *WorldNetDaily*, June 4, 2009, http://www.wnd.com/index.php?fa=PAGE.printable&pageId=100071.

[37] "Democrats Show Their Anti-Christian Bigotry," Traditional Values Coalition, February 5, 2009, http://www.traditionalvalues.org/modules.php?sid=3551.

[38] Chuck Colson, "The Reindeer Rule," *BreakPoint*, December 15, 1992, http://www.breakpoint.org/commentaries/1984-the-reindeer-rule.

[39] Joe Kovacs, "Seasons Greetings: Christians Banned," *WorldNetDaily*, December 2, 2002, http://www.wnd.com/news/article.asp?ARTICLE_ID=41724.

[40] "Nativity Scenes Vandalized Nationwide," Catholic League, December 22, 2008, http://www.catholicleague.org/release.php?id=1536.

[41] "Oklahoma Voters Punish Schools for Nativity Removal," Associated Press, December 17, 2004, http://www.firstamendmentcenter.org/news.aspx?id=14560.

[42] "Campaign: Don't Let Grinches Censor Christmas," *WorldNetDaily*, November 11, 2008, http://www.wnd.com/index.php?fa=PAGE.printable&pageId=80802.

Chapter 2

[1] Michael Farrell, "Judge: D.C. Gay-Marriage Vote Would Violate Human Rights Act," *Christian Science Monitor*, January 14, 2010.

[2] Tim Craig, Michelle Boorstein, Carol Morello, "D.C. Council Digs in on Same-Sex Nuptials," *Washington Post*, November 13, 2009.

[3] Ibid.

[4] Michael Farrell, "Judge: D.C. Gay-Marriage Vote Would Violate Human Rights Act," *Christian Science Monitor*, January 14, 2010.

[5] Jason Davis, "Judge Dismisses Case Disputing Jesus' Existence," *Christian Post,* February 10, 2006, http://newsgroups.derkeiler.com/Archive/Soc/soc.culture.australian/2006-02/msg00086.html.

[6] http://www.luigicascioli.eu/traduzioni/en_1.htm.

[7] Hilary White, "Catholic Activist 'Banned for Life' from Publicly Criticising Homosexuality," *LifeSiteNews*, December 13, 2007, http://www.lifesitenews.com/ldn/2007/dec/07121306.html.

[8] Stephen Adams, "'Hate-Crimes' Laws Ultimately Drag Christians into Court," *CitizenLink*, August 3, 2007, http://www.citizenlink.org/CLNews/A000005189.cfm.

[9] "Court Can Undo Harm to Free Speech," *Calgary Herald*, July 28, 2009, http://www.calgaryherald.com/news/Court+undo+harm+free+speech/1835173/story.html.

[10] Timothy J. Dailey, "Political Correctness Threatens Religious Freedom," Family Research Council, http://www.frc.org/get.cfm?i=IF08H01.

[11] Stephen Adams, "The Slippery Slope of 'Hate-Crimes' Laws," *CitizenLink*, August 29, 2007, http://www.citizenlink.org/content/A000005365.cfm.

[12] Simon Caldwell, "Amendment to Protect Free Speech of British Christians Defeated," *Catholic News Service*, January 1, 2008, http://www.catholic.org/national/national_story.php?id=26417.

[13] Jonathan Petre, "Christian Teacher Suspended over Gay Rights Promotion Row," *Daily Mail*, April 26, 2009, http://www.dailymail.co.uk/news/article-1173579/What-makes-think-natural-heterosexual--Christian-teacher-suspended-gay-rights-promotion-row.html.

[14] Stephen Adams, "The World's Most Dangerous Pastor," *Citizen* magazine, March 2005.

[15] Stephen Adams, "'Dead' Europe Still Kicking," *Citizen* magazine, May 2006.

[16] Soeren Kern, "Europe's War on Free Speech," *Brussels Journal*, February 7, 2009, http://www.brusselsjournal.com/node/3788.

17 "Criminalizing Religious Speech," *The Becket Fund for Religious Liberty*, http://www.becketfund.org/index.php/case/101.html.

18 *Wikipedia*, s.v. "Glassroth v. Moore," http://en.wikipedia.org/wiki/Glassroth_v._Moore.

19 Associated Press "Okla. Ten Commandments Monument Ruled Unconstitutional," June 9, 2009, http://www.firstamendmentcenter.org/rel_liberty/%5Cnews.aspx?id=21680.

20 "Marsh v. Chambers," *Oyez*, http://www.oyez.org/cases/1980-1989/1982/1982_82_23.

21 "Good News Club v. Milford Central School," *Oyez*, http://www.oyez.org/cases/2000-2009/2000/2000_99_2036/.

22 "Washegesic v. Bloomingdale Public Schools," *OpenJurist*, http://openjurist.org/33/f3d/679/washegesic-v-bloomingdale-public-schools.

23 "Doe v. Elmbrook School District," *Americans United for Separation of Church and State*, June 3, 2009, http://www.au.org/what-we-do/lawsuits/archives/doe-v-elmbrook-school.html.

24 "Santa Fe Independent School Dist. v. Doe," *Oyez*, http://www.oyez.org/cases/1990-1999/1999/1999_99_62.

Chapter 3

1 "Obama Nixes 'Jesus' at Georgetown," The Catholic League, April 16, 2009, http://www.catholicleague.org/release.php?id=1596.

2 Chelsea Schilling, "Outrage! *Crucifixes* Appear at Catholic University," *WorldNetDaily*, February 11, 2009, http://www.wnd.com/index.php?fa=PAGE.view&pageId=88609.

[3] Vince Haley, "Save the Wren Chapel," *National Review Online,* November 17, 2006, http://article.nationalreview.com/?q=NTk3Njc2MWM5OWNjZmY3MmNjYzUzMGJiNjZlZWFiY2E=.

[4] "University Newspaper: God Tells Mary, 'You're F----d,'" *WorldNetDaily*, March 17, 2008, http://www.wnd.com/index.php?fa=PAGE.view&pageId=59240.

[5] Bob Unruh, "Prof Calls Student Fascist B------'" *WorldNetDaily*, February 13, 2009, http://www.worldnetdaily.com/?pageId=88723.

[6] Alex Murashko, "Judge Rules in Favor of LACC Student Defending Traditional Marriage," *Los Angeles Examiner,* July 15, 2009, http://www.examiner.com/x-7814-LA-Church--State-Examiner~y2009m7d15-Judge-rules-in-favor-of-LACC-student-defending-traditional-marriage.

[7] David French, "More on Viewpoint Discrimination," Foundation for Individual Rights in Education, April 6, 2005, http://www.thefire.org/index.php/article/5506.html.

[8] "Christian Legal Society v. Newton (UC Hastings)," *Christian Legal Society*, http://www.clsnet.org/content-page-teaser-link/christian-legal-society-v-newton-uc-hastings.

[9] Luke Sheahan, "Religious Liberty Finally Secure in the University of Wisconsin System," Foundation for Individual Rights in Education, February 5, 2007, http://www.thefire.org/article/7707.html.

[10] Julie Foster, "Christian gGroup 'Redeemed,'" *WorldNetDaily*, May 17, 2000, http://www.wnd.com/news/article.asp?ARTICLE_ID=17884.

[11] "Traditional Values Coalition Condemns CA University for Forcing Campus Christian Group to Compromise Beliefs and Statement of Faith," *Traditional Values Coalition*, December 19, 2005, http://www.traditionalvalues.org/modules.php?sid=2543.

12 "University Cuts Off Christian Fraternity," *WorldNetDaily*, August 15, 2004, http://www.wnd.com/news/article .asp?ARTICLE_ID=39975.

13 "Christian Fraternity Fights University Non-discrimination Policy," *The Lookout*, November 28, 2004, www.lookoutmag. com/pdfs/846.pdf.

14 "University 'Bias' Plan Can Get You Busted," *WorldNetDaily*, November 3, 2007, http://www.wnd.com/news/article .asp?ARTICLE_ID=58487.

15 Samantha Harris, "Speech Code of the Month: Northern Illinois University," Foundation for Individual Rights in Education, August 2009, http://64.49.244.212/spotlight/scotm/.

16 Ibid., "Speech Code of the Month: New York University," Foundation for Individual Rights in Education, June 2009, http://64.49.244.212/article/10701.html.

17 "Prof Put on Leave for Using Student in Political Agenda," *WorldNetDaily*, November 17, 2006, http://www.wnd.com/ news/article.asp?ARTICLE_ID=52987.

18 Bob Unruh, "'Toxic' Environment After Christian's Complaint," *WorldNetDaily*, April 11, 2007, http://www.wnd.com/ news/article.asp?ARTICLE_ID=55130.

19 Bob Unruh, "UCLA Student Told She Can't Say 'Jesus.'" *WorldNetDaily*, http://www.wnd.com/index.php?fa=PAGE .view&pageId=100314.

20 Alan Sears, "UCLA Gives Thankful Student Some Latitude for Gratitude," June 23, 2009, http://www.faithandfreedomsunday .net/issues/religiousfreedom/default.aspx?cid=4987.

21 "UCLA Repents of Banning Jesus from Graduation," *Becket Fund for Religious Liberty*, June 9, 2009, http://www

.becketfund.org/index.php/article/1059.html?PHPSESSID=ef124
51eef797c7d93391f6de563fc75.

[22] Roberta Combs, "High School Student Erica Corder Has First Amendment-guaranteed Religious Rights," Christian Coalition, March 13, 2009, http://www.cc.org/blog/high_school_student_ erica_corder_has_first_amendmentguaranteed_religious_rights.

[23] Press Release: "Liberty Counsel Argues High School Valedictorian Case at Tenth Circuit Court of Appeals," *Liberty Counsel*, March 11, 2009, http://www.lc.org/index .cfm?PID=14100&PRID=788.

[24] "Judge Approves University's Viewpoint Discrimination," *WorldNetDaily*, August 12, 2008, http://www.wnd.com/index .php?fa=PAGE.view&pageId=72232.

[25] Alyssa Farah, "'Friend or Foe' Fights Graduation Gagging," *WorldNetDaily*, April 27, 2009, http://www.wnd.com/index .php/index.php?pageId=96382.

[26] Art Moore, "Ads Target Campus 'Anti-Christian Bigotry,'" *WorldNetDaily*, April 15, 2003, http://www.wnd.com/news/ article.asp?ARTICLE_ID=32060.

[27] Tom Jacobs, "10 Supreme Court Cases Every Teen Should Know," *New York Times Upfront*, September 15, 2008, http:// www.nytimes.com/learning/teachers/featured_ articles/20080915monday.html.

[28] "Religious Freedom and Public Schools," *Koinonia House*, August 18, 2009, http://www.khouse.org/enews_ article/2009/1500/.

[29] "Guidance on Constitutionally Protected Prayer in Public Elementary and Secondary Schools," *U.S. Department of Education,* February 7, 2003, http://www.ed.gov/policy/gen/guid/ religionandschools/prayer_guidance.html.

30 Julia Duin, "School Prayer Charges Stir Protests," *Washington Times,* August 14, 2009, http://washingtontimes.com/news/2009/aug/14/criminal-prayer-case-stirs-protests/?feat=home_top5_shared.

31 Ken Connor, "Religious Liberty Stops at the Schoolhouse Door," *Townhall,* June 14, 2009, http://townhall.com/columnists/KenConnor/2009/06/14/religious_liberty_stops_at_the_schoolhouse_door.

Chapter 4

1 Francis A. Schaeffer, *Trilogy: The God Who Is There* (Wheaton, IL.: Crossway, 1968/1990), 8.

2 Ken Connor, "Bread and Circuses: America's Cult of Celebrity," Center for a Just Society, July 3, 2009, http://www.centerforajustsociety.org/press/article.asp?pr=5174.

3 Andrea Brown, "Young Man's Trip to Afghanistan Kills Stereotypes," *Gazette* (Colorado Springs), August, 17, 2009, http://www.gazette.com/articles/afghanistan-60318-space-stephenson.html.

4 Christian Film & Television Commission Staff, "Moviegoers Prefer Morally Uplifting Movies," ASSIST News Service, http://legacy.pastors.com/RWMT/article.asp?ID=194&ArtID=7974.

5 *Wikipedia,* s.v. "Nikos Kazantzakis," http://en.wikipedia.org/wiki/Nikos_Kazantzakis.

6 "Martin Scorsese's *The Last Temptation of Christ,*" *Public Broadcasting Service,* http://www.pbs.org/wgbh/cultureshock/flashpoints/theater/lasttemptation.html.

7 Kathleen Kinsolving, "Celebrating *The Last Temptation of Christ*'s Fifteenth Anniversary," *Scorsese and His Films,* http://www.scorsesefilms.com/lasttemptation.htm.

[8] Michael Medved, *Hollywood vs. America* (New York: Harper-Collins, 1992), 46.

[9] Ibid., 41.

[10] Albert Mohler, "Deciphering *The Da Vinci Code*," *AlbertMohler.com*, April 12, 2006, http://www.albertmohler.com/commentary_read.php?cdate=2006-04-12.

[11] Ibid.

[12] "Cardinal Urges Da Vinci Action," *BBC*, May 8, 2006, http://news.bbc.co.uk/2/hi/entertainment/4750283.stm.

[13] "The Da Vinci Code," *Box Office Mojo*, http://www.boxofficemojo.com/movies/?page=main&id=davincicode.htm.

[14] *Wikipedia*, s.v. "The Holy Blood and the Holy Grail," http://en.wikipedia.org/wiki/The_Holy_Blood_and_the_Holy_Grail.

[15] Albert Mohler, "What Should We Think of the Emerging Church?" AlbertMohler.com, June 29, 2005, http://www.albertmohler.com/commentary_read.php?cdate=2005-06-29.

[16] "Bill Maher: Christians Have Neurological Disorder," *WorldNetDaily*, February 18, 2005, http://www.wnd.com/news/article.asp?ARTICLE_ID=42906.

[17] *The View*, April 19, 2007.

[18] Richard A. Serrano, "Wife of Nominee Holds Strong Anti-abortion Views," *latimes.com*, July 21, 2005, http://articles.latimes.com/2005/jul/21/nation/na-wife21.

[19] Anti-Defamation League, "American Attitudes on Religion, Moral Values and Hollywood," October, 2008, http://www.adl.org/hollywood_poll_2008/.

[20] Steven Greydanus, "Is Hollywood Anti-Catholic?" *Christianity Today*, May 12, 2009.

Chapter 5

[1] Zogby International, "67% View Traditional Journalism as 'Out of Touch,'" February 27, 2008.

[2] Frank Newport, "Church Attendance Lowest in New England, Highest in South," Gallup, April 27, 2006.

[3] Pew Research Center, "2007 Survey of Journalists," December 3, 2007.

[4] Ibid., "Bottom-Line Pressures Now Hurting Coverage, Say Journalists," May 23, 2004.

[5] "Now That Walter Cronkite Has Passed On, Who Is America's Most Trusted Newscaster?" *Time*, July 21, 2009, http://www.timepolls.com/hppolls/archive/poll_results_417.html.

[6] "Mister Christian," *Comedy Central*, January 15, 2001, http://www.thedailyshow.com/watch/mon-january-15-2001/mister-christian.

[7] http://thinkexist.com/quotation/does-anyone-know-does-the-christian-persecution/365748.html.

[8] Don Feder, "Christians Eat Lions in 2004 Election," donfeder.com, http://www.donfeder.com/articles/New%20Folder/bite.doc.

[9] "Survey: Americans Believe Religious Values Are 'Under Attack,'" *Anti-Defamation League*, November 14, 2008, http://www.adl.org/PresRele/RelChStSep_90/5392_90.htm.

[10] Jon Meacham, "The End of Christian America," *Newsweek*, April 4, 2009, http://www.newsweek.com/id/192583.

[11] Albert Mohler, "Transforming Culture: Christian Truth Confronts Post-Christian America," albertmohler.com, http://www.albertmohler.com/article_read.php?cid=1.

[12] David Van Biema, "Christianity's Image Problem," *Time*,

October 2, 2007, http://www.time.com/time/nation/article/ 0,8599,1667639,00.html.

[13] 2 Corinthians 2:15–16 NIV.

[14] Jim Rutenberg, "Media Talk; AOL Sees a Different Side of Time Warner," *New York Times*, March 19, 2001, http://www .nytimes.com/2001/03/19/business/mediatalk-aol-sees-a- different-side-of-time-warner.html.

[15] L. Brent Bozell III, *Weapons of Mass Distortion: The Coming Meltdown of the Liberal Media* (New York: Crown Forum), 107–8.

[16] Phil Brennan, "The Media and Hollywood War Against Christianity," *NewsMax.com*, October 2, 2003, http://archive .newsmax.com/archives/articles/2003/10/2/102405.shtml.

[17] Ibid., 109–10.

[18] John Leo, "Nasty and Sick Propaganda Now Masquerading as Art," *Gainesville Sun*, October 5, 1999.

[19] "New York Times Opines on Bigotry," *Catholic League,* 10/24/2008, http://www.catholic.org/national/national_story .php?id=30220.

[20] "Comedy Central Perpetuates War on Christmas," *Catholic League*, December 24, 2008, http://www.catholic.org/national/ national_story.php?id=31252.

[21] Bob Norman, "Plumbing the Depths of the Christian Tali- ban," *New Times*, August 29, 2002, http://www.browardpalm beach.com/2002-08-29/news/de-regier/.

[22] Brennan, "The Media and Hollywood War against Christianity."

Chapter 6

[1] Zogby/O'Leary Report—4/24/09 thru 4/27/09 MOE +/- 1.6 percentage points.

[2] "U.S. Religious Landscape Survey: Religious Affiliation—Diverse and Dynamic," *The Pew Forum on Religion & Public Life*, February 2008, 1, http://religions.pewforum.org/reports#.

[3] Ibid.

[4] Ibid., 6.

[5] Ibid., 8–9.

[6] Ibid., 38.

[7] Ibid., 39.

[8] Brian J. Grim and David Masci, "The Demographics of Faith," America.gov, August 19, 2008, http://www.america.gov/st/peopleplace-english/2008/August/20080819121858cmretrop0.5310633.html.

[9] Ibid.

[10] Ibid.

[11] Ibid.

[12] Ibid.

[13] Religious Landscape Survey, 62–64.

[14] Ibid., 68.

[15] "Runaway Christian Convert to Stay in Florida for Now, Judge Rules," *Fox News*, August, 21, 2009, http://www.foxnews.com/story/0,2933,541540,00.html.

[16] Frank Newport, "This Easter, Smaller Percentage of Americans Are Christian," Gallup, April 10, 2009, http://www.gallup.com/poll/117409/easter-smaller-percentage-americans-christian.aspx.

[17] Ibid.

[18] Ibid.

[19] Lydia Saad, "Church-Going Among U.S. Catholics Slides to Tie Protestants," Gallup, April 9, 2009, http://www.gallup.com/poll/117382/church-going-among-catholics-slides-tie-protestants.aspx.

[20] *Zogby/O'Leary Report*, 4/24/09 thru 4/27/09 MOE +/- 1.6 percentage points.

[21] Ibid.

[22] *Zogby/O'Leary Report*, 11/7/08 through 11/13/08 +/- 1.4 percentage points.

[23] *Zogby/O'Leary*, 4/24/09.

[24] *Zogby/O'Leary*, 4/24/09.

[25] "56% Disagree with Obama's Comments on Small Town America," *Rasmussen Reports*, April 14, 2008, http://www.rasmussenreports.com/public_content/politics/elections2/election_20082/2008_presidential_election/56_disagree_with_obama_s_comments_on_small_town_america.

[26] "77% Say Inauguration Should Begin with Prayer," *Rasmussen Reports*, January 20, 2009, http://web1.rasmussenreports.com/public_content/politics/obama_administration/january_2009/77_say_inauguration_should_begin_with_prayer.

[27] "66% Say Christmas Is One of the Most Important Holidays," *Rasmussen Reports*, December 20, 2009, http://www.rasmussenreports.com/public_content/lifestyle/holidays/december_2008/66_say_christmas_is_one_of_the_most_important_holidays.

[28] "Easter Poll: 76% Believe Jesus Rose from the Dead," *Rasmussen Reports*, April 6, 2007, http://www.rasmussenreports

.com/public_content/lifestyle/holidays/easter_poll_76_believe_
jesus_rose_from_the_dead.

[29] "Peter Ferrara: The Freedom of Religious Expression
Amendment," *American Civil Rights Union,* December 9, 2007,
http://www.theacru.org/acru/the_freedom_of_religious_expre/.

[30] Ibid.

Chapter 7

[1] *Philosophy and Public Policy Quarterly*, 29, no. 3/4 (Fall
2009): 10.

[2] Ibid., 142.

[3] Ibid., 169.

[4] *West Virginia v. Barnette*, 319 U.S. 624, 644 (1943).

[5] Jonathan Todres, Mark E. Wojcik, Cris R. Revaz (Ardsley, NY:
Transnational Publishers, 2006).

[6] American Bar Association, Center on Children and the Law:
*Children's Rights in America: UN Convention on the Rights of
the Child Compared with United States Law*, 182.

BRAD O'LEARY serves as chairman of the PM Group and publisher of the *O'Leary Report* (www.OLearyReport.com).

He is the executive producer or producer of numerous television specials and films, including *The Planet Is Alive*, an ecumenical movie chronicling the life of Pope John Paul II. This groundbreaking film aired on Russian television on December 24, 1991—the first time a religious program was ever aired there.

O'Leary also conducts numerous charity projects in Vietnam, where he has worked closely with Vietnam's Catholic Cardinal Jean-Baptiste Pham Minh Man on a number of projects, including the construction of a new seminary in Saigon, the sponsorship of two orphanages, and a school program for the Sisters of St. Vincent DePaul. His charity work in Vietnam first began when he collaborated with the U.S. Conference of Catholic Bishops and Bob Hope on a benefit for the boat people.

More recently, he brought a mission to Vietnam that resulted in 2,000 Vietnamese children receiving hearing aids that allowed them to hear for the first time. It later became a television special titled *The Gift of Hearing*.

O'Leary is also a best-selling author of 15 books, including: *The Audacity of Deceit: Barack Obama's War on American Values*; *Shut Up, America! The End of Free Speech*; and most recently, *America's War on Christianity* and *God and America's Leaders*.